CHINA

ON
Life & Management

by **Sheh Seow Wah**

ASIAPAC • SINGAPORE

Publisher
ASIAPAC BOOKS PTE LTD
996 Bendemeer Road #06-08/09
Kallang Basin Industrial Estate
Singapore 339944
Tel: (65) 392 8455
Fax: (65) 392 6455
Email apacbks@singnet.com.sg

Visit us at our Internet home page
www.asiapacbooks.com

First published November 1998

© 1998 ASIAPAC BOOKS, SINGAPORE
ISBN 981-229-039-7

*Unless stated otherwise, all illustrations in this book
are drawn by WOO SIANG BOON*

Cover illustration by Jeffrey Seow
Cover design by Roy Tan
Body text in Century Schoolbook 11pt
Printed in Singapore by Kin Keong Printing Co. Pte Ltd

Contents

Acknowledgements

I would like to extend my deepest gratitude and heartfelt appreciation to the following people:

* First and foremost, Ms Jenny Tanjung from Surabaya, Indonesia, for editing the first draft of the manuscript.

* Special thanks to Dr Lee Cheuk Yin, Senior Lecturer, Department of Chinese Studies, National University of Singapore, for reviewing my manuscript and providing very useful and insightful feedback.

* My deepest gratitude to my family members for their moral support and understanding.

* Last but not least, this book is specially dedicated to my late father Mr Sheh Kak Fa.

About the Author

Sheh Seow Wah, BBA, MBA, MSc. (Management), is currently a lecturer in Singapore. Prior to this appointment, he was a change management consultant for a Chinese business conglomerate in Indonesia for more than two years. He also served as a human resource management consultant with one of the Big Six auditing and consulting firms in Malaysia.

Sheh had been a financier-cum-banker for eight years in Malaysia before he joined the consultancy firm. He was then heading the Credit and Marketing Department for a local branch.

He has served as a lecturer and trainer for several private academic institutions for 10 years and has taught management, finance, personnel, marketing and economics for diploma and MBA programmes.

Sheh was conferred a scholarship by the Public Service Department (Malaysia) for the pursuit of his BBA. He was also awarded a research scholarship from the National University of Singapore to pursue his MSc. (Management). His scope of research includes Chinese values and management focusing on small and medium-sized organisations.

Sheh has had several of his articles published in the local dailies in Malaysia, corporate in-house magazines, national and international journals. He is also the author of the book entitled *Chinese Management*.

Preface

Ever since men started living in groups, consciously and unconsciously, they have organised their lives and managed their day-to-day activities collectively. The successful construction of many ancient temples and statues in China were also owing to a combination of effective organisation and management. Although the definition of the term "management" and its development into a discipline came no more than one or two centuries ago, the concept had long been embedded in the mind of mankind.

The practice of management itself covers the whole gamut of collective units: from self, to family, to team, to organisation, to community and to nation. Even though managing a family is quite different from managing an organisation, the underlying principle remains the same — that of trust.

Although the way a person managed his life 2,000 years ago may be different from the way he might do so today, the underlying principle of management remains the same. This is because the "Principle of Life" espoused by the ancient philosopher is conceptually sound and universally applicable. If one can understand and apply this universal principle, it will teach him how to manage his life. This universal principle of managing one's life can also be applied to managing a team, a company or even a country.

The discipline of management has evolved with the development of man. It can also be said that this new discipline of knowledge is actually an old philosophy and wisdom of mankind. Variations in its practice merely reflect the difference of the thoughts and cultural beliefs among the practitioners. In the 21st century, the movement towards a knowledgeable society will certainly continue, if not accelerate. As we advance towards being a more knowledgeable society, the application of philosophy to current knowledge is already apparent.

There have been little empirical studies done to support the relationship between philosophy and management practice. The objective of my book is to correlate, in a practical manner, the rich philosophical thoughts and cultural beliefs of the Chinese with organisational and managerial practices. I certainly hope that this book will be enlightening to current and future management researchers and practitioners, especially those in East Asia.

Throughout China's history, despite the many wars that she has experienced, religion was never the cause of any of them. The reason for this is that those fundamental characteristics of the Chinese philosophy and way of life were based on the "Principle of Humanism". For more than 6,000 years, the Chinese have been significantly influenced by the powerful and mystical philosophy of the *I-Ching* (*Book of Changes*) and subsequently by the teachings of Confucianism, Taoism and Buddhism about 2,500 years ago. These have produced a culture of humanism which makes the Chinese way of life very practical and at the same time, philosophical.

Having carefully studied the *I-Ching*, Confucianism, Taoism and Buddhism, I have discovered their links to today's organisational and managerial practices. I sincerely hope that my efforts will add a new angle, based on the characteristics of Nature and the Natural Law, to the study of management philosophy.

This book begins with the explanation of the "Principle of Unity" followed by four inter-related principles of Nature — the "Principle of Opposites", the "Principle of Cycle", the "Principle of Balance" and the "Principle of Change".

The division of the Principle of Nature into five sub-principles does not imply that they should be treated separately in terms of application. The breakdown is only to help in the understanding of the principle.

Sheh Seow Wah

The Principle of Unity

NOTHING IN THIS Universe stands entirely alone. Everything is related to something else. In fact, everything is a part of a whole. We, as human beings, who have evolved from Nature, are therefore also a part of Nature just like a passing cloud, a tree, a bird or a rock. If we wish to study Nature, we cannot detach ourselves from it. Thus, part of the study of Nature is the study of one's own self.

To understand and learn from Nature, we should constantly relate ourselves to it. The bottom line is that we can only study Nature in terms of relationships and not in isolation. This is the concept of universal oneness. If we want to study the earth, we cannot ignore the rest of the planets in the solar system. By the same token, the solar system is a sub-system of a larger system.

At times, we may have to divide things into parts in order to study them. However, everything will still add up to a whole. When we cut a big whale (the largest mammal on Earth) into two, we will not get two small and cute whales. Dividing things into smaller parts is to assist one to better comprehend Nature. Consider, for instance, "north", "south", "east" and "west". In reality, they do not exist. They constitute a conceptual framework, a product of the human mind, to facilitate our thinking or understanding of our

古之欲明明德於天下者，
先治其国；欲治其国者，
先齐其家；欲齐其家者，
先修其身；欲修其身者，
先正其心；欲正其心者，
先诚其意；欲诚其意者，
先致其知；致知在格物。

Confucius: "If you want to rule the country, first put your house in order; if you want to cultivate your morality, first put your heart right. To put your heart right, you must be sincere."

Excerpt from *The Complete Analects of Confucius Vol 1-3* (comics) illustrated by Jeffrey Seow.

environment and our operating within the environment. This reality that all things are part of a whole is what I mean by the "Principle of Unity" or "holistic thinking".

The Holistic Way of Thinking

A holistic way of thinking does not apply only to the understanding of Nature but also its principles. Scientists have spent years identifying and then researching the atom. The discovery of the atom is a major breakthrough in science. An atom is so minute that it cannot be seen with the naked eye. Yet scientists have described it in definite terms: an atom comprises a proton in the centre with electrons, in orbits, circulating the proton.

If we observe closely how the nine planets in the solar system revolve around the sun in their orbits, it will not be difficult to see Nature operating at both the macro and micro levels. Don't you think the solar system itself resembles a huge atom? This is how the study of the micro level can contribute to the understanding of the macro level. The converse is also true. Discovering the principle at the macro level will also help us understand how things work at the micro level.

The Principle of Unity was first put forth by Lao Zi and then strongly espoused by Confucius. According to Confucius, "If you want to rule the country, first put your house in order; if you want to cultivate your morality, first put your heart right. To put your heart right, you must be sincere." The relationships of an individual begin first with the relationship the individual has with himself, which then evolves into an ever-expanding network of relationships with others.

3

The Collective Mind

The inter-relation of things in Nature and their causalities should be closely studied. All events that occur in Nature have their causes and their effects. This is how all things are related. The collective approach of looking at Nature begins with the recognition that natural and human events follow certain patterns and relationships.

This collective study of events and patterns means to see things in terms of their parts and relationships — to see the forest and the trees, if you will. All human events do not happen in isolation. Each is always linked to some current or seemingly remote incidents of long ago. The power of the mind is its ability to make sense of these events by relating one to the other and thus to create a "picture" in the mind. This ability to use "photographic" visualisation (what to me, is to see things in a three-dimensional fashion) strongly enhances our memory power and our ability to think. The next time you need to remember a long list of household items, try to remember it using pictures instead of words.

Words are among the greatest creations of mankind. However, being a creation of man, this medium of communication is limited. The number of words and their usefulness depend largely on the way man perceives the world, which is also the source of the limitation of words. Words can name the things of Nature, such as a star, the moon or the sun but words cannot fully explain them. Words cannot reveal the true nature of things. If we try to use more words to explain something or a principle in Nature, we cannot get a complete answer. It is important for us to think beyond words and not let our thinking be trapped by our own creation. Where possible, we need to think in terms of symbols, diagrams or pictures instead of just words alone.

Build a multi-dimensional view in our mind. In Chinese philosophy, the use of diagrams such as *Ba Gua* (Eight Trigrams) some 6,000 years ago was to facilitate the understanding of the principles of Nature.

The average Chinese man who has been educated under a Chinese education system normally comes away from that system with several positive attributes such as a good memory, good judgement and an ability to predict well. In a Chinese school, a student is taught to memorise school text books from young. In the long run, this way of learning strongly enhances the memory power of the student.

The characteristic of "collectivity" is observed in the characters of the Chinese script. If you study Chinese characters — which are built from radicals — you will realise that each radical has its own meaning. When they are combined, different meanings will be created. For example, the combination of the radicals 日 (*ri*), which means "sun", and 月 (*yue*), which means "moon", will give rise to the character 明 (*ming*), which means "brightness" or "brilliance". You can also predict the meaning of the Chinese character by reading its strokes. The Chinese character for 山 (*shan*) which means "mountain" resembles the shape of the mountain. By learning Chinese characters, one is able to improve the ability to judge and predict.

The collective mind sees things in terms of relationships and is able to transcend the limitations of language (words and sentences). This ability to see beyond the eye (of things visible and invisible), listen beyond words (beyond sound and silence) and think beyond the language (to think about thoughts) is a great asset that man should acquire.

The Interrelation

Nature teaches us that everything in the Universe are interrelated and interdependent. Every creation, natural or man-made, is not created in isolation. A strong wind that follows a heavy downpour blows the leaves away. Everything is interrelated through cause and effect.

If the members of an organisation do not understand how their jobs are related to one another, there will be confusion and frustration. An organisation is the result of its members' thoughts and behaviours. To be more precise, an organisation is a social entity which captures and classifies its own experiences and events over time. It records knowledge and behaviour in patterns and ties them together in a logical way. An organisational behavioural study basically analyses its members' thoughts and behaviours individually and collectively.

The relationships between organisational events can be briefly classified into positive, negative, curvilinear and uncertain ones. For example, researchers reveal that as task responsibility increases, task performance improves (positive relationship) whereas over-simplification of a task is directly inverse to performance (negative relationship). Of course, the validity of these findings will largely depend on the level of management and the type of organisation concerned. In yet another finding, an increase in work pressure will result in better performance. However, beyond a certain level, as work pressure keeps increasing, performance will deteriorate. This is a curvilinear relationship. Establishing a cause-effect link among the organisational events is not always straightforward because more than two organisational events may need to be observed and they need to be observed over a longer period of time than usual.

The interrelation of events and behaviours are evident in performance management. In an organisation, if every individual in the section does well, the overall section's performance will be good. If every department in the company does well, the company will achieve excellent results. Similarly, if all the companies in a business group perform well, the group will prosper. As stated by Confucius, the prosperity of a nation begins with the individual.

All the departments in an organisation have been created for the purpose of achieving the organisation's goals. Each department should not be treated as a separate entity but be viewed as a part of the whole. In a "4 by 100 metres" race, no matter how fast each athlete runs, if the passing of the baton is not well co-ordinated among all the athletes, the team will never win the race. In the same way, the Human Resource Management (HRM) department should not be a separate unit but should serve and support the Marketing and Operations departments. All HRM programmes should be assimilated into the management system of the line functions.

Human Relationships

Confucius teaches that every individual in a society must nurture and keep healthy five fundamental human relationships or *wu lun* (五伦) for that society to be a stable and peaceful one. These five relationships refer to that between husband and wife, father and son, brother and sister, a sovereign and his subjects, and that between friends. The foundation of these relationships is the cultivation of the self. The benefits of cultivating oneself will gradually

Confucius: "The prosperity of a nation begins with the individual."

自天子以至於庶人，一是皆以修身为本。其本乱而末治者否矣；其所原者薄，而其所薄者厚，未之有也。

Excerpt from *The Complete Analects of Confucius Vol 1-3* (comics) illustrated by Jeffrey Seow.

spread to maintaining good relationships with others.

In Chinese, the word for "country", 国家 (*guo jia*), is made up of the character for "state", 国 (*guo*), and the character for "family", 家 (*jia*). The Chinese believe that an orderly society and country begins with strong and healthy families, the basic building blocks. Hence, the strong emphasis in Chinese culture on the importance of the family and filial piety as the governing force of Chinese vertical relationships (relationships between fathers and their offspring).

The emphasis on the family and the need to always strive to bring honour to the family's good name (and therefore honour to one's ancestors), have made the Chinese most earnest and diligent in matters relating to the family. A diligent person is enthusiastic in nature and will strive to excel in his career or in whatever he does. Likewise, an overriding concern for a stable and happy family leads to a frugal and peaceable lifestyle.

Whether it is in the East or West, in the traditional or modern society, human relationships are the source of the life force and spirit that binds people together. For centuries, the Chinese have subscribed to the system of maintaining and giving "face" as well as "good relationships" (*guanxi*). This system of "giving face" (not snubbing or embarrassing or belittling others) lies at the crux of relationships in the Chinese society. In general, the rules of the game that the Chinese play by are:

"Granting of face" is reciprocated by "gaining of face".

If someone has been gracious and has accepted, for instance, your invitation to an important event, then he has "granted you face". You should then reciprocate when an opportunity arises, by doing something that will make this person look good in whatever circles concerned. If you like, it is like boosting his ego since he has not bruised yours in the first place. Conversely,

"Refusal of face" is reciprocated by "losing of face".

If someone has snubbed you by, for instance, turning down your invitation to an important function, you will, when the opportunity arises, snub him in return.

It is essential for a person who wants to understand *guanxi* to understand the value of "face". Once you have made someone "lose face", it will adversely affect the relationship between you and the person. This "loss of face" will cost you as much as a business deal. Just like trust, it takes a long time to build but just one negative incident is enough to destroy it. Once it is lost, it is extremely difficult to rebuild.

The Natural Instinct

No matter how fierce a tiger, an eagle or a panther, it will never attack and kill its own offspring. If we observe the law of the jungle closely, we will see that an animal will not prey on its own kind. This animal instinct is a good principle to be applied in an organisation.

In an organisation, it is always unhealthy for one department to "attack" another department at the expense of the overall organisation's well-being. There are many reported cases whereby workers deliberately "go slow" or go on strike just to flex their muscles to show management that they can do damage, that they cannot be ignored. But

they must remember that to an entrepreneur, if the demand of his workers for a higher pay does not commensurate with their productivity, then he should liquidate his business and invest elsewhere. In the end, it is the workers who will suffer.

At the industry level, undercutting prices to increase market share is unhealthy. Over the past decades, many companies and countries have suffered badly from price wars. In the long run, price wars "kill" the industry because some of the companies will have to close down and leave the industry. Companies should learn to live in harmony with one another in an industry. Any permanent reduction of price should be an outcome of market forces (demand and supply) or as a result of production efficiency. As price is the main element in maintaining equilibrium in the market economy, it should not be used as a weapon.

Unity is strength. Internal unity and consolidation is the

key to competency which in turn can be built into a competitive edge. Study how one person's job is related to another person's, one department's work to another department's, one organisation's activity to another organisation's and so on. It is important to view things in terms of relationship and maintain the overall harmony.

The Insightful

In a Chinese organisation, the charismatic Chinese leader demonstrates a strong ability to look at a problem from many angles. The insight to see things from all angles and maintain the whole picture allows a Chinese leader to

diagnose the organisation's problem comprehensively before seeking permanent solutions.

A popular Chinese fable has it that a man once gathered five blind men and asked them to feel an elephant and then tell him what the elephant was like. The first blind man felt the trunk and said that an elephant was like a snake; another happened to touch a ear and therefore went on to describe an elephant as being like a big fan. The third blind man touched its body and said that an elephant was like a wall; still another, who happened to feel its leg, thought an elephant to be like a tree trunk. The last blind man who grasped the huge animal by its tail was very sure that an elephant was no more than a thick rope. None of the blind men was able to describe the exact form of the elephant. This story goes to show how not being able to see a situation from different angles leaves you without the truth.

We can see how this situation applies to modern-day context. In pricing a product, the production people will tend to price it against the quality, and the accounting people will price it according to cost-plus methods. The marketing people will price a product based on demand and supply, while an economist will price it based on the price elasticity of demand for the product. But in reality, do you not think that price is a function of quality, cost, competition and elasticity of demand? The ability to see things from all angles and use a holistic approach is a prerequisite to success.

Very often, people from different backgrounds have very contrasting views in defining management theories and concepts. For instance, in defining the word "organisation", an employee views it as a place to work and earn a living as well as a career ladder. From the manager's point of view, an organisation is a structure with various functional activities such as production, marketing, finance, accounting, personnel, information technology, and research and development. A system analyst, on the other hand, defines an organisation as a pure science, an open system which constantly strikes an equilibrium between different sub-systems of inputs, processes and outputs. It is called an open system because an organisation constantly interacts with the environment that it operates in. A business organisation purchases resources (material, human and capital) and processes them so that it in turn sells goods and services to the society. In contrast, a sociologist sees an organisation as a cultural entity which comprises values, norms, beliefs, heroes, rites, rituals, customs and ceremonies. In reality, an organisation is all of the above.

In traditional Chinese medicine, the medication is slower in efficacy compared to Western medication. The Chinese seek to cure and improve the overall health of the patient instead of just focusing on the injured organ. They believe that the functioning of an organ, and therefore its problems, are closely related to those of other organs. As such, in seeking a permanent cure, they use a holistic approach. Here again is an instance of the Chinese being insightful.

Networking

Just as a fishing net is made up of a series of knots, every natural and human event in this world constitutes a network. Since World War II, the Japanese have successfully conquered the world market in just over 50 years. Today, we can find Japanese electronic goods in practically all parts of the world, even in the remote areas of Africa. How did the Japanese achieve this? By establishing a comprehensive distribution networking.

Over the last few decades, the Japanese have not only spent a tremendous amount of time and effort in upgrading their production management but have also made great effort in the distribution of their products. Today, if we choose to compete with the Japanese, we have to compete not just against the high quality of their products and their competitive pricing but also their established far-reaching distribution network. I reckon this to be the biggest challenge in competing against the Japanese.

As documented in Michael Porter's book, *Competitive Advantage*, distribution networks have been identified as one of the main competitive advantages as well as an entry barrier for many successful multinational organisations. It is important to invest sufficient time, effort and money to build and maintain comprehensive networks. In addition, building cordial relationships will further enhance and reinforce the reliability of the business and distribution networks. The Chinese businessman likes to use *guanxi* to reduce their market risk. It is because, during bad times, many Chinese businesses rely on these good relationships (or *guanxi*) and strong networking for survival. Giving a personal touch when it comes to customers, whether from the past, present or of the future, will always be advantageous.

The interrelation of economies and trades will continue to be the major force governing global events. In order for organisations to internationalise their activities, going downstream and building a comprehensive distribution network is necessary. Just as a spider builds a web to define its territory, an organisation should establish its market segments and distribution network to define its battle-ground.

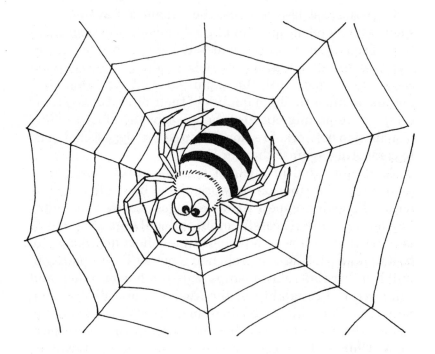

Embracing Self

In Nature, nothing comes into existence only to disappear again. There is, in fact, no clear distinction between existence and non-existence and between being and non-being. Both are parts of the whole. It is only a matter of transformation of state when something, once existent, becomes "non-existent". The coming into existence of a thing is only a transformation of state. No matter how brilliant a human being is, he or she cannot create something out of nothing. All things come from within Nature, including Nature itself. Hence, it is said that the totality of particles in the Universe — the number of matters or atoms — always remains the same.

This universal law of Nature teaches us the limit and opportunity cost for all creation. If you use the resources of Nature to create something, there is always an opportunity cost, that is, you would have to forgo producing alternative goods and services. This what the economist has identified as the principle underlying the discipline and study of economics two to three centuries ago. The discipline of economics is a study of productivity. It is a study of using limited resources (inputs) to produce optimum quantities of goods and services (outputs). The greater the amount of goods and services we produce using the same amount of resources, the better we are at creating wealth.

A housewife with a fixed monthly income should learn to economise so that her family can derive the highest satisfaction from it. Similarly, a businessman needs to effectively utilise his limited resources (capital and labour) to optimise his returns by obtaining a good balance between risks and returns. At the national level, a government uses the budget to maximise the economic and social welfare of the people.

The economic success resulting in the good life that we are experiencing today was supposedly not attainable until AD 2000, based on the records and trends of the past. But, because of rapid advancements made in science and technology, the world economy and the overall development of mankind is able to make that quantum leap into today's world. However, there is a hidden price for it.

The greatest challenge facing mankind in the 21st century is an ecological one. Today, economists, politicians, sociologists and environmentalists have to be more ecologically aware than their counterparts of the past. More and more world organisations are taking actions to conserve the natural resources and to protect Nature. Whether it is at an international, national, organisational or individual level, we should continuously learn to manage and use our scarce resources wisely.

Space

The tendency to view things in isolation can lead to disillusionment. We need oxygen to survive, but when we breathe, we inhale nitrogen and carbon dioxide as well. The tangible and intangible aspects of things (likewise, *what it is* and *what it is not*) are both parts of a whole. We should always try to understand and learn about the tangible as well as the intangible aspects.

The value of a house is its land and building materials (bricks, steels, tiles, etc.), but its usefulness is the emptiness or space created by the four walls (the intangible or *what it is not*). Similarly, a good Chinese landscape painting should not fill up the whole canvas. Sufficient space should be provided to allow the viewer to reflect and imagine.

We create space to live in. We should also create space in our minds to think and learn. In order to allow learning to take place, we should first learn to unlearn. If a person's mind is "stuffed" with his own opinions, he behaves stubbornly. The mind is just like a drinking glass — we have to empty it before we can fill it. We should always keep an open mind and be less judgmental when we receive feedback or new information. We need to possess the information first before we attach a value to it. It is commonly observed that many people are flexible in their behaviours but stubborn in their thinking.

It is important to make sense of the tangible (*what it is*) but it is also essential to make sense of the intangible (*what it is not*). When one listens and understands the words as well as the silence, the unsaid becomes apparent.

The Distinction

Not only are all things in Nature parts of a whole, they are also all equal — as far as Nature is concerned. In Nature, an ant is as valued as a tree or a human being. A man is a man only if he treats all men equally. There is no division

or distinction among creation. Whether a country is developed or developing, or a person is good or bad, the sun still shines on them. Nature is neutral in judgement.

Human problems begin when people start to make

distinctions: right and wrong, good and bad, possible and impossible, tangible and intangible. These distinctions are products of the human mind. Those who are caught in these entanglements will suffer. In the history of mankind, the division of the Earth into continents, regions and countries has created much political and economic tension and warfare. Divisions, producing North and South Korea, North and South Vietnam, East and West Germany — just to name a few — have caused much misery to the people in these countries. During the British colonisation of Malaya, the practice of "divide and rule" was used. This strategy suppressed the strength of unity in order that the British could achieve their economic objective of exploiting the rich natural resources.

To make distinctions is to make judgements. In an organisational context, whenever feedback is given, we should focus on the behaviour and try not to judge. If an employee is late for work, we should describe the behaviour by saying, "John was 10 minutes late" instead of saying, "John is lazy". People are more willing to listen and accept feedback when we describe the issue or behaviour and not the person. Avoid being judgmental in whatever you see or hear. Describing a behaviour without imputing a value is particularly important in effective communication.

As long as we unnecessarily distinguish things and then attach a value to them, trouble lies ahead of us. Always be detached and see things from a holistic point of view. Nothing is created in isolation and without its usefulness. Learn to hold two or more contrasting views at the same time without discriminating against them, always bearing in mind that all things are created equal.

The Leverage

To discover the principle — or principles, since they are all interrelated — of Nature, we can use both micro and macro approaches. Very often, a micro study of nature may lead to a major discovery or breakthrough. For example, the study of a leaf is linked to the study of a tree trunk and its roots, which in turn leads to the study of the soil, the earth and the great creation of all beings including animals, birds, fish and human beings. A microscopic study of a leaf could uncover a macro principle of Nature. This is the concept of leverage.

Complex as a thing may seem, it can be understood with fundamental scientific principles. According to Einstein, it is upon a simple principle of Nature that one thing can evolve into thousands and millions of other things and events. It takes but a single cell to evolve into a complex living organism. This phenomenon is consistent with the principle of Tao in which Tao produced the One, which then multiplied into tens of thousands of things.

An old Chinese proverb says,

"It takes four ounces of effort to lever a thousand pounds" (四兩拔千斤), which means if one is wise enough, one has only to use a little effort to gain great advantage and obtain great results. The same idea lies behind the modern saying which says that "working smart is even more important than working hard". While it is important for a person to work hard in order to be successful, working hard alone is simply not enough. One must also learn to work smart.

In order to work smart, one must fully understand the kinds of activities that one is going to perform. Firstly, one must prepare a definition of each activity and determine the workload using time or cost criteria. Classify the activities into primary or secondary and value-added or non-value-added activities. Then study how one can reduce or eliminate those secondary and non-value-added activities. For secondary activities that only support an organisation's primary objectives, reorganise and simplify them. As for non-value-added activities, which are of least importance where the achievement of organisational goals is concerned, eliminate them as far as possible.

It may be difficult to imagine how the whole process works but through continuous self-introspection, clarity of mind and commitment, nothing is impossible. Some Chinese proverbs put it thus:

The journey of a thousand li begins with one single step.
千里之行，始于足下。

Most events start with a difficult beginning.
万事开头难。

A good start is 50 percent towards success.
好的开始是成功的一半。

There is no such thing as a difficult task unless there is lack of determination.
世上无难事，只怕有心人。

With respect to business, leverage is commonly practised in financial management. In today's business, no businessman will finance his business with solely his own capital. A wise businessman also uses the concept of leverage to enhance his asset base. For example, for every single dollar invested in the business, a businessman will borrow another two or three dollars to finance its assets. In financial terms, it is called financial leverage or gearing ratio. As a rule of thumb, a gearing ratio of 1:1 is considered healthy which means for every single dollar invested, a businessman should borrow the same. However, in reality, it is common for businesses to lever at a gearing ratio of 2:3.

The higher the financial leverage or gearing ratio, the higher will be the financial risks. For example, with a gearing ratio of two times, a businessman who has invested $1 million will be able to raise $2 million of borrowed funds and hence possess an asset base of $3 million. The higher the asset base or productive assets (resources), the greater will be the production capacity and earning power. In this manner, the businessman can obtain higher returns. But the businessman also bears a higher risk of becoming insolvent. Well, higher risks, higher returns!

The Discovery

To learn and discover from Nature requires one to study and investigate Nature from which knowledge is derived. Scientists took decades to discover several major break-throughs such as the Law of Gravity, the Law of Action and Reaction, and the Law of Forces. How did they do it? They did it with a probing mind. It is important to probe deeply and to investigate things with an open mind. In thinking deeply about a matter, one needs to be unbiased and fearless. This is the spirit of science.

Being able to keep an enquiring or open mind is a necessary quality in identifying organisational problems. Always ask five to seven questions for every problem you encounter and you will soon get to the root of a problem. In Japan, it is believed that a problem properly defined is itself the solution.

The ability to probe in great detail will help identify the real cause of a problem and not just the symptoms. This is a good principle to follow: a problem that is properly defined is 50 percent solved.

If a staff is frequently late for work, try asking the following five questions:

Why have you been frequently late for work recently?
Possible Answer: Because I can't catch the bus.

Why can't you catch the bus?
Possible Answer: Because I wake up late.

Why do you wake up late?
Possible Answer: Because I sleep late.

Why do you sleep late.
Possible Answer: Because I have to moonlight.

Why do you have to moonlight?
Possible Answer: Because I do not earn enough money
for my family.

It could well be that you are not paying your employees adequately. Perhaps it is time to review the current salary package and benchmark it against the industry's standard. Remember, identifying the problem only solves 50 percent of the problem; the remaining 50 percent comes from the solution.

The Strategic Mind

The Chinese strategic mind is very much the result of its study of Nature. The beautiful landscape and scenery of China is a rich source of inspirations. It is commonly noted that the Chinese often use their observations of Nature to develop their strategic thinking.

All cultures have their own wise sayings. The study of any culture will be incomplete if we do not study these sayings. The study of the proverbs of a particular culture or race would enable one to better understand its philosophy and way of life.

In the Chinese culture, proverbs are known as "common sayings" or *shu hua* (俗 话). Although many of these sayings have not been properly organised and documented, they have been passed down from one generation to another by word of mouth. They have also been quoted in many Chinese books. The Chinese common sayings cover all aspects of the Chinese life. They range from human behaviour and relationship to education, wealth, business and spiritual matters. Because of their wide coverage, they can be used as a source of guidance throughout one's life.

One of the most famous and widely known documentations in the Chinese civilisation is *Thirty-six Stratagems*. Each stratagem consists of four Chinese characters used for different purpose and situation. Very often, the stratagems are applied in human diplomacy and business competition. The following three stratagems are extracted from *Thirty-six Stratagems*:

Stratagem 13

Beating the grass and alarming the snakes.

25

打草惊蛇 *(da cao jing she)*

Debrief: In business, before launching a major marketing strategy, conceal it from your competitors. Otherwise your competitors may copy and launch it earlier.

Stratagem 15

Excerpt from *Thirty-six Stratagems* (comics) illustrated by Wang Xuanming.

Lure the tiger to leave the mountain.
调 虎 离 山 *(diao hu li shan)*

Debrief: In business, it is at times important to distract your competitors and then launch a surprise attack.

Stratagem 20

Excerpt from *Thirty-six Stratagems* (comics) illustrated by Wang Xuanming.

Catch a fish in troubled waters.
混 水 摸 鱼 *(hun shui mo yu)*

Debrief: In order to strike at competitors and catch them unaware, we should first create confusion and trouble to distract them.

It is apparent that the above three stratagems were derived from observations of the animal world. Indeed, many Chinese common sayings were inspired by Nature. In short, the emergence of the Chinese civilisation over the past 5,000 years must have been a result of observing and studying Nature. Nature is, after all, the wellspring of the civilisation of mankind. Even as we pursue rapid advances in science and technology, we must not forget to stay close to Nature so as to enrich our souls.

Heaven's Will

The mind-expanding discoveries of the laws of Nature by major physicists such as Isaac Newton (the laws of motion and gravity) and Albert Einstein (the general theory of relativity) conform with ancient philosophy. These discoveries have also been used to put in perspective events of the past and present as well as to predict the future.

Newton's law of motion says that if an object is moving in a straight line, it will continue to move in like manner forever unless a force acts upon it. Similarly, if an object is at rest, it will be motionless unless and until a force outside of it acts upon it. This law of motion also states that every action is followed by an equal and opposite reaction.

According to Einstein, everything in Nature has been defined in relation to another. An object is said to be big as long as we can find something smaller than it, and vice-versa. It is a matter of relativity. This phenomenon is also applicable to motion, speed and gravity as expounded by Newton.

From the very moment the Universe was formed and set in motion, it will continue in this fashion. The entire phenomenon is a huge self-perpetuating system which is predetermined or fated. This explanation is in line with Newton's law of motion. The Chinese called it "Heaven's will" or "Heaven's decree".

No matter how intelligent man is in creating sophisticated devices to study and measure the Universe, we must not forget that these devices are derived from Nature itself. It is impossible for man to be able to completely comprehend Nature and the Universe. We cannot use the properties of Nature to describe and explain Nature. To some degree, man can only define his own reality in accordance to how he perceives Nature. In Eastern philosophies such as Buddhism and Taoism, the notion of reality (which embraces space and time) only exists in the state of consciousness. If everything in Nature is predestined, then how can man determine his own destiny?

From the macro perspective, the Universe is predestined or fated to exist. But the micro events of people are not. According to the Chinese, it is predestined that one person should know another person since the probability that one individual will meet another particular individual is one

* affinity

out of six billion (the size of the world's population) or 0.000000017%. However, whether the relationship between these two persons will develop and progress after that predestined initial meeting will largely depend on their will instead of Heaven's will. Living within this predestined world, there is still plenty of space and opportunity for man to exercise his will in fulfilling his dreams and aspirations.

The Golden Rule

Lao Zi, an enlightened master, was a man of very few words. He believed that silence is golden. He believed that a lot of things in the world are better left unsaid rather than risk having them explained or spoken of wrongly. An enlightened person, Lao Zi believed, always lives in a mindful state.

It is existence that creates the concept of time and space. As explained by Buddha, "Consider the candle which we light and then subsequently blow out. Where does the flame come from and where does it go to?" Existence and non-existence are part and parcel of the whole. When we are born, we exist in Nature; when we die, we do not get out of Nature. Life and death are always from within.

Life and death are not opposites. All life comes from within. It is from nothingness that life begins. Life begins with one cell and gradually grows into a being. Upon death, a body will gradually decay and decompose into one cell and then back to nothingness. Whatever principles that hold true for Nature must also be applicable to human beings and vice-versa. Intense space research has also revealed the existence of black holes where everything will go back to nothingness and it is from nothingness that everything evolved.

Life is like a mirror. The more we know about Nature, the more we know about ourselves. The principle of Nature is the reality of ourselves. Not only is everything part of everything else, everything contains everything else. Therefore, one way to study and understand Nature is to study and understand the self. Instead of looking outward to study Nature as most scientists do, we should be continuously looking inward to discover the realities.

The golden rule is to embrace all there is in life — the "positives" and the "negatives". In order for one to transcend time and space, one must learn to embrace life and death, being and non-being, beauty and ugliness, good and bad, right and wrong, and so on and so forth as they are NOT opposite forces but part and parcel of the whole. This is what I mean by the universal wholeness or oneness.

Summary of Learning Points

✔ Everything is a part of a whole. We can only study Nature in terms of relationships and not in isolation. This is what is meant by "holistic thinking".

✔ All natural events in the Universe follow a certain pattern and relationship.

✔ Mind power is the ability to make sense of events by relating one event to another and then forming a "picture" in the mind.

✔ Unity is strength. Internal unity and consolidation is the greatest fundamental competency from which a competitive edge can be built.

✔ Human relationships are the wellspring of the life force and spirit that binds society together.

✔ The ability to see things from all angles and maintain the whole picture is one of the attributes of a successful Chinese business leader.

✔ In order for organisations to globalise their activities, going downstream and building a comprehensive distribution network is necessary.

✔ In the Universe, nothing appears and disappears. Similarly, there is no clear distinction between existence and non-existence, between being and non-being. Existence is a state in a process of transformation.

✔ The totality of the particles in the Universe always remain the same.

✔ The discipline of economics is the study of how to use and allocate the scarce resources in Nature effectively.

✔ Learn to use the tangible (*what it is*) as well as the intangible (*what it is not*) aspects of all things.

✔ All things in Nature are created with equal importance. There is no division or distinction among them. Nature in itself is free of judgement.

✔ A micro study of Nature may lead to a major discovery or breakthrough. This is called the concept of leverage.

✔ Nature is the wellspring of the civilisations of man. In pursuing rapid advances in science and technology, we must not forget to stay close to Nature so as to continually enrich the soul.

✔ The discovery of the principles of Nature requires a probing mind.

✔ Through continuous study of man's nature, the principles of Nature will be revealed.

✔ From the very moment the Universe was formed and set into motion, a self-perpetuating system has been created and will continue in this motion. The Chinese called it "Heaven's will" or "Heaven's decree".

✔ Silence is golden. A lot of things in the world are better kept unsaid than risk being falsely explained.

✔ An enlightened person always lives in an awakened or a mindful state.

✔ The golden rule is to embrace everything in life.

The Principle of Opposites

THE COMMON PRINCIPLE underlying all relationships and events is derived from the way of Yin and Yang forces. The fluid, soft and feminine force is the Yin property whereas the hard, rigid and masculine is the Yang force. The origin of the concept of Yin and Yang comes from the concept of oneness. Originally, there was but one force which then became two — the Yin and the Yang. When the two are combined, many are created.

All matters in the Universe possess material forces which comprise both the Yin and Yang properties. According to Taoism, all creations are a combination of these two forces. Nature creates human beings from its own forces and when we die, we return to Nature. It is this material force of Nature that has brought about physical beings like the tree, animal and human being. This transformation process may take many lifetimes. Although it has been said that every event in the Universe has its cause, the ultimate cause is always kept unknown.

In a family, the husband represents the Yang and the wife represents the Yin; and the father is the Yang while the child is the Yin. In an organisation, the employer is the Yang and the employee is the Yin. In an economy, the international and national levels are the Yang (macro) and the industry and organisational levels are the Yin (micro).

The Force of Harmony

Yin and Yang are opposite forces. Although both forces function differently, the two are mutually dependent. A husband depends on the wife as much as the wife depends on him. In a family, the parents depend on the children as much as the children depend on the parents. Similarly, the employer depends on the employee as much as the employee depends on the employer. The two forces should be integrated and each should work for the benefit of the other.

In an economy, the supplier depends on the consumer as much as the consumer depends on the supplier. Under the first and the second law of economics, the forces of demand and supply depend on each other. Economic problems (either inflation or recession) only arise when demand is not equal to supply. When demand exceeds supply, the prices of goods and services increase and cause inflation. On the other hand, when supply exceeds demand, the prices of goods and services decline and cause business failures and the result is recession or unemployment. Hence, it is important for the two forces to harmonise with each other. The common factor that harmonise demand and supply is price.

In order to ensure universal peace, the Yang must be in harmony with the Yin. Peace prevails when there is harmony between husband and wife, employer and employee, and a government and its people. Otherwise, peace or equilibrium will not exist. This is the universal law.

Yin

Water is fluid and soft (the Yin) but it will wear away stone, which is rigid and hard (the Yang). As a rule of Nature, whatever is fluid and soft will overcome whatever is rigid and hard. Similarly, a young plant (the Yin) is small and fragile, but flexible and yielding. On the other hand, a mature plant (the Yang) is huge and strong, but stiff and brittle. When there is a heavy storm, it is the mature plant that will break and die, whereas the young plant will bend and flex back to its original position.

In terms of management theory and practice, planning, organising and controlling are always known as the "hardware" (the Yang) whereas directing and staffing are called the "software" (the Yin). The ability of the management to execute its plan (the Yang) is guided by inner wisdom (the Yin). A manager may be able to plan well, create effective organisational design and install comprehensive control system and mechanism. However, he will not be effective in the long run if he or she partially or totally fails to use the "software", which includes staffing the right people, motivating and directing them through an effective leadership style.

Similarly, a martial-art expert uses a right combination of hands and legs (the outer tools or the Yang) coupled with internal strength (the inner resource or the Yin). Much has been written in Chinese martial-art stories that if an exponent has great internal strength, he can hurt his opponent using only a leaf.

Management practitioners should learn how to strike a balance in using the hardware and software of management tools. In fact, a leader's effectiveness depends heavily on his ability to attract, select, motivate and retain good people in his organisation. That is to say, the Yin controls the Yang.

Let me illustrate further how Yin controls Yang. Unlike an ordinary tree where the tree trunk is strong and hard when matured, a bamboo tree is flexible but strong. When a strong wind blows, the bamboo tree bends but gradually flexes back. In Taoism, we call this "strength within softness" or flexibility.

A leader uses authority, rules and regulations as well as a system of incentives and disincentives to control the behaviour of his subordinates. These management tools are very useful in helping a leader get a task done. On the other hand, if he relies too heavily on them, he becomes helpless when these tools lose their effectiveness.

In contrast, a wise leader never relies solely on modern management tools. His subordinates are fully motivated, possessing enthusiasm and commitment. A truly great leader is able to harness the virtue of his weapons without being controlled by them. In addition, a wise leader uses powerful speech and psychological approaches to motivate his subordinates. Like a bamboo tree, a wise leader is soft or diplomatic in his approach yet firm in his principles.

The Flexible Organisation

The principle of Yin and Yang is not only applicable in management but in business and organisation theories as well. All organisations grow from small to medium size — before they grow large. While it is important for organisations to enjoy economies of scale, they should also concurrently maintain their flexibility. They will otherwise face the fate of a mature plant: breaking easily in the face of difficult situations. An organisation should learn to strike a

balance between size and flexibility.

Korean businessmen normally adopt the policy of being Number 2 in position instead of Number 1. This is because competitors tend to focus their attention and energy on counteracting the strategies of the Number 1 competitor while neglecting the Number 2 competitor. Just as a small bird admires how high a big bird flies, it forgets that the higher a bird flies, the greater the chance of it being shot down by a hunter. As an old Chinese proverb says, "Large trees trap more wind"(树 大 招 风), which means that the larger the organisation, the more likely it is to attract the attention of the public.

Over the last few decades, Chinese family business organisations have grown many times without gaining much attention from the public. This is because Chinese business organisations always keep a low profile and are active only in supporting industries. The medium-size Chinese business organisations are highly flexible and resistant to economic recession. Do you know the average return on investment (ROI) of a medium-size Chinese business organisation compared to a large organisation? Some studies have revealed that the ROI of a medium-size business organisation is higher than that of a big one.

Dinosaurs disappeared from the Earth due to their enormous build. Over the last decades, many large multinational organisations were compelled to retrench and downsize. It is evident that a huge organisational structure is burdensome as it results in bureaucracy, procrastination and overall inefficiency. If communication has to go up and down the hierarchy, business gets lost and the organisation gains a bad reputation for its unresponsiveness to customers' needs.

In today's organisation, we are talking about a non-hierarchical structure or "flat" structure. Middle management that adds no value to the organisation should be eliminated. Organisations that maintain a hierarchical structure will be less able to meet the demands of a changing environment. Organisational structure needs to be "flat" in order to react promptly to a changing environment and be ready to capitalise on any opportunity arising in the environment. A well-maintained fluid structure enables the organisation to adapt well to its environment and continuously re-invent and re-engineer itself for excellence.

We are moving from a "command" structure created one century ago to a flexible structure. Maintaining a highly fluid organisational structure is a MUST and not an option. The high degree of involvement by the cross-functional team members provides various kinds of expertise in the strategic planning process, in managing new projects, and more importantly, in enhancing total customer value. Having the right mix of people in the sales team is highly essential to enhancing customer support and winning a service deal.

Being large is not necessarily beautiful. Neither is being small. When your business is too small, you cannot influence market trends and prices. Being medium-size is the best because it enjoys the advantages of being large and small. This is why it is the global trend of businesses to stay medium in size.

The Middle Way

The dual approach of looking at events is observed in organisational theory. In terms of management, too much specialisation of tasks is as bad as no specialisation. When a task is broken down into numerous small and simplified activities, it becomes boring. On the other hand, job specialisation brings about efficiency and higher productivity. In tomorrow's management, a job will no longer be divided into small and simplified activities performed by individuals. The trend is that it will be performed by work teams. An average of five to eight individuals with diverse expertise will group together to perform a job. Upon completion, the team will be dissolved and each individual will be re-assigned to a different task in a different team.

The same goes for too much centralisation against over-decentralisation of power. A great deal of centralisation will facilitate control but it will greatly contribute to bureaucracy and retard the decision-making process. On the other hand, over-decentralisation may result in the abuse of power and hence contribute to white-collar crimes.

In tomorrow's world, more people will rely less on position or legitimate power based on the organisational hierarchy. As we gradually move towards a knowledgeable society, knowledge or expertise will soon become the main source of power. Besides, as one person's task is significantly correlated with the task of another person, the use of social power increases. This will strongly enhance teamwork, co-ordination and co-operation within the organisation.

In effectively managing people, the use of power to influence and stimulate the right behaviour is crucial. For instance, people are afraid of tigers because they kill. If a tiger's teeth and claws are extracted, will people still be afraid of it? Not likely since all that's left is a big cat.

In an organisation, people are afraid of the leader because of his power to reward and to punish. If these two powers were to be taken away from the leader, would people still be afraid? After all, if a worker makes a mistake, the leader would no longer have the power to punish; on the other hand, if another worker does something right, he cannot reward him either. Reward and punishment are two very powerful management tools to influence people's behaviour and performance.

These two powers are used daily in management practices as well as in annual performance appraisal exercises. The performance appraisal exercise not only provides the platform for superiors to communicate their expectations and performance feedback to their subordinates, but also serves as an opportunity for them to exercise their authority to reward and punish. Therefore, it is important for the management to learn how to use its authority wisely. It should be used to get better results and NOT for an ego trip.

At the infant stage of an organisation's life-cycle, the formulation of procedures and policies are rare. There is a marked tendency to treat all past and present decisions made by the organisational leader as a matter of policy. In the absence of clear work procedures and policies, much time is spent "putting out fire", resulting in stress, frustrations and embarrassments.

On the other hand, there is a tendency for a large and mature organisation to be over-circumscribed by too many procedures and policies. Red tape and bureaucracy are the common illnesses suffered by a large organisation.

Rather than swinging from one end of the spectrum to the other, it is suggested that the "Middle Way" — that of not being too large or too small — be taken.

The Coin

The concept of opposites exists only in our mind. When we recognise that something is good, the opposite — evil — becomes defined as well. The way we perceive the surroundings will naturally give rise to the opposite. There are two sides to a coin but there is only one coin. Opposites co-exist in unity. A common saying among the Chinese is, "Water keeps a boat afloat but can overturn it as well"(水 可 載 舟, 亦 可 覆 舟). In the exploration of Nature, many initial theories and concepts seem to oppose each other but in reality they complement each other.

Money is one of the greatest inventions of man. Money, as we generally know it, comprises notes and coins. Under the barter trade system, there must be a double coincidence of wants in the buyer and seller for exchange of goods and services to take place. With the creation of money, the new system allows a person to buy now and sell at a later period and vice-versa. Money becomes a major facilitator in all transactions in the economy. The faster the money circulates, the higher the volume of economic activity. Money also makes international trade a reality. Through international trade, countries benefit from their differential advantages and enjoy a wide variety of goods and services. Hence, our quality of life has improved tremendously with the invention of money.

However, the love of money is also the root of all evils. If people work only for money, then society becomes highly materialistic. Money is like opium. Once addicted, we long for more and more and soon forget the purpose of life. We will focus only on the accumulation of wealth as the main pursuit in life. We often think that by earning more money, we win the "battle" against the rest of the players in the market. However, if we think deeply, we will come to the realisation that the "battle" is within oneself. We must not forget that a human being is both a material and spiritual entity.

From the economic viewpoint, the creation of money is the main cause of two major economic problems: inflation and recession. In a barter trade system, the buyer has to meet the seller before a transaction can take place. Hence, demand is always equal to supply because one has to buy and sell at the same time. However, under the monetary system, one can buy now and sell later and vice-versa. Thus, aggregate demand is not necessarily always equal to aggregate supply. When demand exceeds supply in the economy, it causes price to go up, resulting in inflation. On the other hand, a situation of excess supply causes the price to decline, possibly leading to business failure. A recession may then result.

Everything that is conceptualised by human beings has its advantages and disadvantages. A wise person learns to maintain the balance between the good and the bad rather than strive to eliminate the bad and cultivate the good. We should carefully understand the extremes but practise moderation. It is the practice of moderation that immunises one from the harmful effects of the extremes.

The Complementary

Over the past centuries, the independent and investigative nature of the Westerners has enabled them to forge many breakthroughs in science and technology. To the West, it is man who controls the physical world and not the other way round. The breakthroughs by the Western world have greatly benefited the development of mankind and improved tremendously its economic welfare. As a result, before World War II, the Western economies were a century more advanced than the economies in Asia.

For thousands of years, a metaphysical approach was used in trying to understand Asia. To Asians, man plays only a small part in Nature which has existed long before the evolution and civilisation of mankind. Asians respect Nature but in a passive way. They have exerted as much energies as the people of the West in exploring Nature. However, the superstitious nature of the Asians has led to their falling far behind the West in the development of science and technology.

If the findings of the West are properly combined with the rich philosophical thinking of the Asians, do you not think that a great source of synergy, capable of great discoveries and breakthroughs, would result? In the Chinese script, the combination of the character for the word "East" (*dong*, 东) with the character for the word "West" (*xi*, 西) will give rise to the word *dong xi* (东 西), meaning "objects". The future will be guided by our ability to balance the use of Western science and Asian philosophy.

In management principles, Western management style emphasises "rights and responsibilities" (the Yang component) whereas the Asian style relies more on "relationships and values" (the Yin component). In reality, both are equally important for organisational effectiveness.

With regard to leadership, courage, charisma and discipline (qualities which constitute the "hard" image) are considered the requisites of an effective leader of the West. On the other hand, the Asian leaders emphasise qualities like wisdom, patience and tolerance (the "soft" image). Again, in practice, both qualities of "hard" and "soft" images are essential to effective leadership.

In managing organisations of the future, a combination of Asian and Western philosophies, theories, principles and techniques will be ideal. For over 50 years, Asians have learned much from the Westerners where science and technology are concerned. From now onwards, the reverse should take place, that is, the Westerners should learn Asian philosophies and wisdom.

Theory X and Theory Y

In the 1950s, Douglas McGregor put forth theories, known as Theory X and Theory Y, for explaining human nature. According to McGregor, how a manager treats his employees depends on his view of human nature.

Under Theory X, it is assumed that employees by nature are lazy and dislike work. Hence, they have to be coerced to perform in their jobs. In order to increase labour productivity, the Theory X manager uses monetary incentives, division of labour, rigid work procedures, strict rules and hierarchical structure.

On the other hand, under Theory Y, it is advocated that employees by nature like to work and are committed to achieving an objective. They always seek responsibility in their jobs. The Theory Y manager constantly uses non-monetary incentives, cross-functional exposure, flexibility and freedom, and an effective reward system to bring about overall efficiency.

These two theories are akin to the Chinese view of man, a view which is several thousand years old. And the view is that man has two natures or two sides inherent in him. He is naturally good and at the same time naturally evil.

In China, Shi Huang Di, the first emperor of China, subscribed to Han Fei Zi's philosophy in ruling the country. Han Fei Zi, born around 280 BC, was a scholar of Chinese political science. He crystallised his thoughts in some 55 essays. Han Fei Zi believed man to be naturally evil, for whom strict rules and severe punishments are needed.

The following are some tenets of Han Fei Zi's philosophy (which comes under the school of Legalism):

- A ruler's position in any matter is always justified by his power to reward and punish. Thus, he should not share too much of his power to reward and punish with his ministers. A ruler should rule his people through the exercise of his authority and the administering of laws.

- Those who violate the laws should be punished; those who obey the laws should be rewarded.

- Man is self-seeking by nature. Hence, man's conduct needs to be guarded by law and codes of behaviour.

- In the eyes of the law, all men are equal. No man, not even a prince, is above the law.

- In formulating a law, the penalty for breaking that law has to be severe to deter anyone from violating that law.

- In implementing the law, there must be absolute enforcement. No man must be considered to be above the law.

There is a Chinese saying that goes thus: "We need to punish the one in order to warn the hundreds." (杀一以儆百) In other words, the Chinese leader believes that in order

to ensure the effectiveness of the law, he must enforce it by punishing the few so as to warn the multitude that the law — and its enforcement — is real.

In contrast, Confucius and Mencius believed man to be by nature kind and good. The Confucianists maintain that people should be ruled by proper rules of conduct and morality. Based on the assumption that man's nature is good, one would be able to cultivate a person's character and train one's personality through proper education (at home and in school).

Confucius was not in favour of using punishment. According to him, if we were to govern people by laws and thus regulate their venality, this is not conducive to inculcating a sense of shame in them. On the other hand, if we lead people by virtue, by exhorting them to virtue and being exemplary in character, and then have them guard their actions with proper rules of conduct, they will develop a sense of shame and hence become good citizens. Confucius further added that it is not necessary to punish a person who breaks the laws just to remind the law-abiding ones. The actions of a person, Confucius believed, are the product of his heart's desire. In the words of Confucius, "If a gentleman desires to be good, he will naturally be good." (我 欲 仁, 斯 仁 至 矣) Confucius was very good at gently leading a man to the path of virtues or persuading him to observe those codes of conduct becoming of a cultured person.

The Legalists, as we see, subscribe to Theory X and the Confucianists to Theory Y.

In modern management, the development of an effective control system and rules and regulations to support organisational and economic effectiveness are indispensable. However, the human aspect should not be overlooked. If an effective legal or control system alone can manage and control human behaviour, there would be no crime and other kinds of social problems. Although effective laws and rules are important in guiding human behaviour, they do not automatically improve people's morals.

If the relationship between management and employee is not well established, it will be disastrous to over-emphasise the punishment or disciplinary system. It is only strong positive social influence and a good education system that will ultimately change, reform and shape the behaviour of the people.

The Total Brain

The human brain can be studied by dividing it into two halves or hemispheres: the right side and the left side. These two sides function differently. According to psychologists, the left side of the brain possesses the ability to think logically and rationally, and it perceives the world in a linear and causal way. On the other hand, the right side of the brain thinks irrationally, emotionally and tends to accept the world the way it is — it does not judge or analyse what it perceives. The Yin and Yang concept is a metaphor for the workings of the right and left sides of the brain.

In our modern society, most people reflect a left hemisphere orientation. They think thus: Today is Friday, now is 3:00 pm and tomorrow I will go to the beach. Time is a left-brain phenomenon. This explains why modern man is so stressed out trying to fulfil deadline after deadline. It is the left side of the brain which controls and dominates over the right side of the brain in day-to-day affairs.

Let me illustrate how the whole brain is used in decision-making. Making effective and good decisions is one of the most important responsibilities of a manager. However, very few managers are trained to do this. The following describes the five steps of a decision-making process:

Step 1: Define the problem
Step 2: Generate alternatives
(use the right side of the brain)
Step 3: Evaluate alternatives
(use the left side of the brain)
Step 4: Choose the best alternative (use the whole brain)
Step 5: Implement the selected alternative and evaluate results

It is important for one to identify a problem correctly before moving on to the next step of the decision-making process.

Creativity is the most important element in generating both practical and yet innovative alternatives. Use your right brain (to think divergently) to generate alternatives or ideas. In the process of generating ideas, allow your brain to run a little wild — go outside the conventional rules or boundaries. The following are idea killers which should be avoided in alternatives or ideas generation:

- It won't work here.

- We've tried it before and failed.

- The management won't go for it.

- It is too costly and not within our budget.

- We're not ready for that.

In screening the alternatives, convergent and logical thinking (which requires the use of the left side of the brain) are involved in the whole process called analysis. Some of the methods that can be used to systematically evaluate all the alternatives are decision-tree, cost-and-benefit analysis and returns-on-investment.

Finally, when it comes to choosing the best alternative, the whole brain (for both divergent and convergent thinking) is involved. Certain criteria for decision should be developed. The criteria might involve, for example, the following:

- Amount of time needed to implement the selected plan, and for benefits or results to show

- Cost of implementation of the plan

- Quality of the alternative, and expected level of resistance or acceptance of the plan by employees

- Ethical considerations

- The primary impact and repercussions of implementing the plan

In implementation, it is essential to define the level (or levels) of management which will be involved and its (or their) degree of involvement. In some cases, it is important for the top management to be involved in the implementation stage to increase the likelihood of success of the plan.

It is important for one to learn to make use of the whole brain effectively. We should carefully understand the functions of both hemispheres of the brain and maintain a balance in the use of the two hemispheres of the brain.

The Limit

Every element in Nature has its limits. A pillar can be used to support the roof of a house but if the roof is too heavy for the pillar, it will collapse. If we over-exploit Nature — stretching it beyond its limits — it will react. An instance of Nature reacting to our abuse is the hole in the ozone layer. Work within the limits of Nature and it will not harm us.

The economic growth and development of mankind over the past 50 years has been recorded as one of the highest in history. However, as a result of over-exploitation of the natural resources of the earth, ecological problems arise. Ecological issues will be the major problems facing mankind

in the future. Mankind must learn to balance its needs with those of Nature, and respect its limits. Knowing when to say enough is the first step towards understanding limits.

On the other hand, ecological constraints can be treated as opportunities. One person's loss is another person's gain. Countries and organisations that control major energy and natural resources will greatly benefit from the present global scenario.

Even as we understand the advantages and disadvantages of extremes (such as centralisation versus decentralisation, formalisation versus non-formalisation, and structured versus unstructured organisation), we should, in practice, observe moderation. In the economic sphere, too much interference from the government is as bad as no governmental interference. Similarly, the ruling party should choose the best mix between economic growth and economic development. High economic growth without proper economic development (poor distribution of wealth) leads to long-term political instability. Be very conscious of extremes and practice the "Doctrine of Moderation".

The Absolute

There are no absolutes in Nature. When we describe attributes of things in Nature, it is always in relation to something else. In reality, there is no human being who is absolutely good or bad. Even the "best" person in the world possesses certain negative attributes. Similarly, no matter how bad a person is, there is always some good in him. In Taoism, this is known as the Yin within the Yang and the Yang within the Yin. If you were to study the Yin-Yang diagram, you will see that it consists of the black and white portions. But within the black portion there is a white spot and vice-versa.

The principle of Yin and Yang is highly relevant to organisational events as well. In business dealings, no

matter how trustworthy the other party is, we still need to put things in "black and white" — that is, spell out terms of the agreement in writing — in order to protect all parties concerned. Similarly, when implementing a strategy within an organisation, do not only focus on its primary benefits. Think about its secondary impact, especially the negative ones. It is because no matter how perfect a plan or strategy is, there are always some loop-holes or defects. There is always that spot of black in the white.

The Yin and Yang principle can be positively utilised. Both the strengths as well as the weaknesses of a person can be useful. Similarly, both the rich resources of Nature as well as its wastes can be utilised.

The Contradiction

It is my prediction that at the turn of the next century, developed and newly-industrialised countries will experience another new stage of evolution of mankind. It will be a revolution, the effects of which would be just like those of the industrial revolution which took place one and a half centuries ago. The future will not bear the image of the past. It is my belief that whatever holds true today will be proven to be of the contrary in the future.

In AD 150, a theory was put forward that the Earth was located in the centre of the Universe and that the rest of the planets moved around the Earth in their orbits. That theory was held for about 1,000 years until 1543 when Copernicus "correctly" — since this truth may also be displaced — placed the sun in the centre of the solar system. This phenomenon is a classic example of the "Principle of Contradiction".

A century ago, the wages of a general worker was based

on piece-rate basis. Over the years, it has gradually evolved from piece-rate to time-based and from a seven-day work week to a five-day work week. Today, many organisations are reversing the reward system by suggesting that employees be paid based on work done instead of time spent.

Things have changed and will continue to change. Not only has the reward system evolved from what it was to what it is today, the performance appraisal system is also taking on a new orientation. Soon the traditional top-down appraisal system cannot stand alone in appraising a person for effectiveness and performance. It will need to be reinforced by a bottom-up appraisal system with the subordinates appraising their direct superiors.

The "Principle of Specialisation" espoused by Adam Smith was practised for more than three centuries. If organisations still remain highly specialised, can they meet the demand of today's sophisticated consumers? It's time to rethink specialisation, and to reorient the business organisation from one focused on production to one being customer-focused. Today, we talk more about cross-functional teamwork, networking structure and matrix organisation. The principle of specialisation that emphasises individual performance and self-achievement will no longer be relevant to our changing society.

In terms of economic effectiveness, natural resources used to be ranked number one followed by capital resource among the four factors of production, the other two being labour and entrepreneurship. Today, a well-informed and skilful workforce is the major competitive edge. Companies that still fail to recognise and value human development will lose out in the competition. This is why policies on education or the design of education systems continue to be the major focus of many political leaders.

In the past, economists identified thriftiness and a high saving rate as an important engine of growth for an economy. The paradox is that consumption instead of investment is the driving force today.

One thing is clear. Change is not going to be a linear equation anymore. Besides talking about the speed of change, from now onwards, the additional focus is on directional and quantum leap change. The future will bear hardly, if at all, any resemblance to the present.

Relativity

In the study of Nature, reality is relative, not absolute. Everything in the Universe, whether big or small, beautiful or ugly, good or bad, right or wrong, black or white, tall or short is described thus relative to one another. It is always difficult for scientists to describe their findings of Nature in absolute terms. Everything has to be defined in relation to another. It is meaningless to define things in absolute terms. For example, when scientists describe the force of gravity on earth, they have to explain it in relation to the force of the cosmos. Explaining things in relation to other things while keeping the whole picture constantly in view are pre-requisites for the acquisition of more knowledge.

In the organisational context, if an organisation is described as big, how big is it? Compared to what is it big? Similarly, if the work performance of an employee is said to be "the best", then we must also find out the performance of the others. This "Principle of Relativity" as espoused by Einstein, also referred to as "benchmarking", is the most recent management tool.

As the concept of benchmarking is derived from the

principle of relativity, the meaning of benchmarking can be defined or interpreted in many ways. A literature review has revealed that there are more than 50 definitions. For the purpose of understanding, benchmarking can be referred to as an on-going, systematic and organised effort to evaluate an organisation's performance, based on certain criteria for the purpose of organisational effectiveness and improvement. Benchmarking covers a wide range of organisational activities which include the organisational mission and strategy, system and work process, market and product profile, as well as competitor analysis. The assessment process cuts across all functional units including production, marketing, research and development, accounting and finance, information technology, and personnel and administration. The whole process includes data collection, data analysis, designing improvement program, implementation and evaluation.

This information collection and assessment process is a continuous process and the entire investigation may be tedious and quite labour-intensive. However, in the long run, it will allow the organisation to develop a comprehensive database which can be used to identify areas of weaknesses and performance gaps, and generate solutions and action plans for organisational improvements.

As we move forward from the industrial age to the information age, more and more business decisions will be based on figures and not feelings. In the 21st century, information will be the fuel for the human mind. The more relevant information is made available, the better will be the quality of decisions made. Thus, organisat-ions should continuously benchmark their practices against their competitors' and their industries' best practices, including functional best practices domestically and globally.

The Principle of Relativity is a moving constant, which means to say the constant movement or change of time provides a new dimension in perceiving reality. It is sometimes called the fourth dimension. What has been said to be big today, may just be found to be the opposite the next day. Nothing keeps its status quo. In understanding this principle, an organisation should never take things for granted but instead, benchmark itself against the best performer of the industry domestically and internationally. In today's business, organisations should not assume that what is best today will do well tomorrow. Very often, the factor that brings you success now may also be the factor that brings about failure. The reality is that many of our problems today arise from the success or successes of our past.

Organisations should continuously use benchmarking as a diagnostic tool to measure and manage its performance. They should never leave anything to chance. All organisational events and outcomes should be the result of planned efforts.

Cause and Effect

The law of Nature teaches us that for every action, there is an opposite and equal reaction. This law, a major contribution to the development of science, was discovered by Isaac Newton. In the East, the "Law of Cause and Effect" espoused by Buddhism speaks the same truth but in a different context. All these boil down to a very basic analogy, that is, nothing happens by chance because nothing can happen without a cause. Every event is the effect of a cause and is itself the cause for another event or effect.

It has also been said that the problems we face today are caused by our past actions. Knowing and understanding the consequences of our actions will enable us to better manage our lives. Similarly, in an organisation, we should start by planning what we want and then work towards achieving those goals. This goal-oriented philosophy is not new to us. In fact, it has been introduced and made popular in the West since the 1950s and is known as "management by objective" (MBO). The effectiveness of this concept is unquestionable. What we need to do is to study how we can effectively introduce this goal-oriented concept into our management system.

The philosophy of MBO not only provides the business organisation with a vision but also has deep meaning for the individual. Employee participation in the setting of organisational objectives enhances the individual's motivation and sets the criteria for performance. The individual becomes more effective in planning his work, time management and performance. The achievement of the individual work objectives then contributes directly to achieving departmental objectives and together with other departments' achievement of their work objectives, enables the organisation to achieve its organisational goals.

Setting objectives or goals is the driving force behind the progress of all business organisations. Although each member of the organisation comes from a different familial, cultural and educational background, they must all contribute towards a common purpose, that is, profit maximisation. Organisational objectives become the common baseline and an effective instrument that co-ordinate and pull together the efforts of all in achieving the performance goal of the business.

The implementation of MBO philosophy requires management to be very focused, consistent and persevering in their management of time and effort. Commitment and support from top management is a MUST. The leader of an organisation needs to effectively make this MBO philosophy the foundation of the management system and help its people to apply it in their thinking and behaviour. In the long run, a truly effective organisation is one where all individual efforts are welded into a common effort.

The Seed

If we plant apple seeds, we will get apple trees which bear apples. Similarly, if we plant orange seeds, we will get oranges. In managing people, it is also important to understand what we work into the mindset of our people. If we plant the right kind of values, we will get the desired behaviours. If we plant the wrong values, it will be translated into different types of undesirable behaviours.

Organisations should carefully identify and select the right set of values and encourage their staff to inculcate these values. These values can either be borrowed from their own social environment or created from top management's vision. In today's modern management terminology, it is known as "corporate culture".

In the past, most corporate leaders used creative structural design, effective systems and control mechanisms to encourage and draw individuals at all levels towards translating an organisation's vision and goals into reality. But such systems are inadequate today. For any long-lasting organisational change to be sustained, a fundamental change of its cultural values and norms is required.

Not only do cultures exist in all types of organisations, it is imperative for the organisational leaders and entrepreneurs to know and understand them. The long-term prosperity of an organisation is often attributed to its strong organisational culture as this is a powerful lever for guiding the behaviour of employees. The converse is also true: the corporate culture can also bring about the failure of an organisation.

The stronger the culture, the richer and more complex the value system. Consider this: the first and most basic value of Matsushita Electric in Japan is "Matsushita Electric is a company that makes people". To Matsushita Electric, they must first develop good people before they can make good products and have a thriving business.

In order to successfully make certain corporate values and norms a part of an organisation, it is necessary to strike a balance between three modes of diffusion: communication, behavioural and system modes. The corporate values and norms need to be continuously communicated to all existing and new employees. Management personnel should espouse the values and be role models through daily interaction with the staff. Cultural values and norms should be built into the management system and reflected in the performance appraisal and reward criteria. Employees who demonstrate these behavioural norms should be appropriately rewarded. When people are promoted, recognition should be given to the fact that they have been exemplary of the corporate values and norms.

The process of diffusion and assimilation of certain values into the culture of an organisation can be expected to be extremely difficult and tedious, but it is certainly worth the efforts. Through persistency, it has been observed, corporate values and norms soon become the most important core competency of an organisation.

At the macro economic level, cultural values have been sought to explain the economic dynamism of the "four dragons" of East Asia, namely South Korea, Taiwan, Hong Kong and Singapore. Although political, governmental and economic factors have been identified for the economic effectiveness of these four dragons, they are grossly inadequate. It will be too general to classify the political and economic environments of these countries as identical. If political and economic factors were adequate in explaining the economic efficiency of these countries, how did these various Chinese ethnic groups (basically under the influence of Confucianism), living in different political, economic and social environments, achieve economic success in about the same period? When political and economic factors failed to provide a complete explanation for the economic success of these countries, the importance of the cultural factor came to light. It was seen that having the "right " cultural values will greatly facilitate the implementation of the governmental economic policy and the process of economic growth and development.

The Fluid Properties

The properties of water (Yin) can be related to the qualities of an effective leader. Natural law is neutral in judgement, just like water which refreshes all things in Nature without distinction and judgement. This is its nature.

Similarly, a wise leader should possess the qualities of water which effortlessly nourishes everything in Nature. A wise leader should pay careful attention to all people surrounding him without being possessive, biased or coercive. As the saying goes, "The success of a person does not depend on how many servants he has, but on how many persons he serves." Just as water flows from a high point to a low point, a wise leader should be humble enough to serve the majority with a high sense of equity and justice.

When the water in a lake is still and clear, it naturally reflects all images. This is another natural characteristic of water — it is transparent and reflective. In pursuing infinite material comforts, we often forget to be still and quietly reflect on our past and current activities. We are often either too engrossed with our daily work, leaving little time for reflection, or we conveniently forget about it.

An effective leader consistently puts aside 15 to 30 minutes toward the end of the work-day to quietly reflect on the day's activities. Such a quiet time allows us to look inward (self-introspection) and slowly digest what has

happened throughout the day. It is also a time for all our senses to rest. Inner peace is a great source of energy.

Then there's another great wisdom one finds in water. A wise leader does not intervene his group's work unnecessarily. He believes in playing the role of a facilitator, facilitating the group's process and not his own process. He does not force his own wishes, ideas and insights on the group. Like the transparency of water, a truly great leader is almost invisible. When a team successfully completes a task, they will say, "We did it by ourselves." As the saying goes, "How much a leader can achieve is unlimited for as long as he does not mind who ultimately gets the credit."

The Principle of Life

Nature is a living organism in which everything is

governed by the Principle of Life. In a broad sense, everything in Nature is a living thing although the evolutionary process may differ from one thing to another. Nothing in Nature can be considered dead.

All human beings go through the cycle of life: birth and death. But the Principle of Life does not end when a person is dead. It is crucial to understand that even a dead person is governed by the Principle of Life. Once a person is dead, the body will not immediately stop changing but continue to act according to this principle: decaying and decomposing. This process will continue indefinitely. Hence, a living man and a dead man are both governed by the same Principle of Life. However, there is a distinct difference between the two in that the former is governed by both the Principle of Life as well as the spirit of life. Similarly, the only distinction between a man and a stone is that the former possesses a living spirit but the latter does not.

With this Principle of Life, man can be viewed in two ways. On the one hand, man can be defined as a human being living in this physical world for the purpose of learning and practising to be spiritual. On the other hand, man can be defined as a spiritual being living in this physical world to learn and practise to be human. Between these two ways of looking at man and the purpose of his being on earth lies the difference between a philosopher and a religionist. Confucius, the philosopher, certainly was of the latter point of view. In his teachings, Confucius dealt very little with the subject of life after death. To Confucius, life is pre-destined by Heaven. Practically all of Confucius' teaching of benevolence (*ren*, 仁) is about the practice of humanity. It is only through the continuous practice of humanity that a man may be called a gentleman (*jun zi*, 君子). In contrast, a religionist begins with defining man as a human being and is of the understanding that it is through earnest practice and devotion that he will become a spiritual being.

To Lao Zi, the body and the soul are not two separate entities but one. Dividing life into body and soul is a dangerous assumption. According to Lao Zi, it does not matter if man is defined as a human or spiritual being. He is a strong believer in naturalism — that man should live in harmony with Nature, following its principles in his life.

It is human nature to divide or categorise things. For example, it is said that Westerners are more materialistic while the Easterners are more spiritual. Similarly, some choose to group all the Westerners as individualists and the Easterners as followers. Such distinctions can never be correct. It is always best to accept things as they are. This is the best principle in life.

Free Flow

To follow in the footsteps of Lao Zi is to understand and accept life as it is. Lao Zi led a simple life without complaining or questioning life. In fact, no one knows the real name of Lao Zi. In Chinese, the meaning of the word "Lao Zi" literally means "the old guy". He was an old man who lived to a very advanced age but the dates of his birth and death remain unknown. Lao Zi believed in being natural. To him, whatever can be explained by words is only superficial reality. No words can possibly explain the truth. The meaning of life can only be experienced.

From the viewpoint of Lao Zi, Nature is morally free or neutral in judgement. Not only are all things in Nature parts of a whole, they are also all equal. There is no division or distinction. Whether a nation is developed or less developed, or a person is good or bad, the sun still shines on them. There is no such thing as "natural justice" which is only a matter of human perception. Morality is only relevant for people who are immoral. The way we think can only give rise to opposites. Similarly, when one perceives something as beautiful, the term "ugly" arises. Judging always creates opposites. The world will be moral and beautiful only if people stop judging or completely forget about the terms "moral" and "beautiful".

When we judge, we claim to know better. And when we claim to know better, it boosts our ego and we act arrogantly. If we claim not to know better, then we stay humble and become wiser. In this sense, Lao Zi's philosophy is to think "nothingness". He believed that to practise Tao is to unlearn what we have learned in the past. In reality, what is meant by knowing something in this most undefined and uncertain world? By pointing at the moon and saying we know it is not true. All we have done is merely remember the name of this object that we have seen before and named.

Man uses his five senses to perceive his surroundings and in turn uses his reasoning powers to understand them. This is precisely what a scientist does. How and how much one can perceive and understand one's surroundings is very much subject to one's ability to use one's senses. For example, if one cannot see the colour blue, one's mind will be unable to know what blue is. Hence, one is unable to explain part of this reality. What we can think logically and reasonably depends on what our senses can perceive. Everything boils down to this fundamental principle: the state of everything in the Universe is subjective, not objective. Even man himself stands relative to everything else in Nature.

Thinking and knowing do not make a person perfect. Lao Zi believed in *wu wei* (无 为) or "doing nothing" or "noninterference". This principle of *wu wei* is also shared by Confucius in *The Analects* which suggests, "To have done nothing (*wu wei*) and yet the country is well-governed and in order." Both Lao Zi and Confucius believed that the best way to govern a country is to interfere the least possible. In the scientific study of Nature, scientists call this the Principle of Least Action. Some scientists believe that in studying and understanding the laws of Nature, the harder one pushes, the further from reality will the results be.

Live life as it comes, the way water follows its natural course. Do not favour anything or take sides but accept life as it is. This may sound simple to many people, but in practice it may be very difficult to carry out. Learn to embrace everything in life — the good and the bad, the right and the wrong. Remember, everything is not only part of everything, but everything also depends on everything else. Be detached and resigned.

Summary of Learning Points

✔ The common principle underlying all relationships and events is derived from the way of the Yin and the Yang.

✔ Yin stands for qualities that are fluid, soft and feminine while Yang stands for qualities that are hard, rigid and masculine.

✔ All creations are a combination of the two material forces, Yin and Yang.

✔ Yin and Yang are opposite forces but mutually dependent.

✔ Yin will ultimately control Yang.

✔ A great leader is guided by both the inner strength (the Yin) and the outer force (the Yang).

✔ Maintaining a highly fluid organisational structure instead of a hierarchical structure is a MUST and not an option if a highly successful organisation is desired.

✔ The formation of cross-functional teams is the trend for today's management so as to function effectively.

✔ With regard to specialisation, delegation of power and formulation, the "Middle Way" is the ultimate solution.

✔ Effective laws and rules are important in guiding human behaviour, but they do not automatically make people more moral or ethical.

✔ Always work within the limit, and Nature will not work against us.

✔ There is no such thing as "absolute". Everything is a matter of relativity.

✔ Nothing happens by chance because nothing can happen without a cause. Every event is an effect as well as a cause for the next event.

✔ Nature is always fair. We reap what we sow.

✔ A wise leader should possess the qualities of water and tirelessly serve as many people as possible.

✔ Water is reflective and transparent. A great leader always practises contemplation. He intervenes the least and keeps a low profile. He is almost invisible in his leadership style.

✔ In a broad sense, everything in Nature is a living thing although the evolutionary process may differ for each.

✔ To emulate Lao Zi is to be detached and resigned to everything that comes to one in one's life. The meaning of life can only come from experience.

The Principle of Cycle

NATURE ALWAYS FOLLOWS a cycle. As such, things are never constant but are changing all the time. For instance, the leaf that drops from the tree decays in the soil and is absorbed by the roots as nutrients and subsequently reproduced as new leaves The cycle continues for years and even when the entire tree dies, the cycle continues.

In Chinese philosophy, there is the concept of the Five Elements — Metal, Wood, Water, Fire, Earth (金, 木, 水, 火, 土). These elements are commonly known as the five processes of the whole, which describe the interaction of elements in the physical or material world.

In the generative cycle of the Five Elements, these five elements are interrelated in a specific order. The inter-relationship between the five elements can be explained thus: Fire burns the Wood and turns it into ashes. Upon accumulation, these ashes form the Earth where Metal is found. When Metal is melted at a certain temperature, it is transformed into liquid, representing Water. Water nourishes all things on earth, including the trees which in turn provide the Wood. This natural cycle is endless.

Before the formation of the Earth, it took millions or even billions of years for the mass in the Universe to evolve, transform and condense. The whole process of condensation

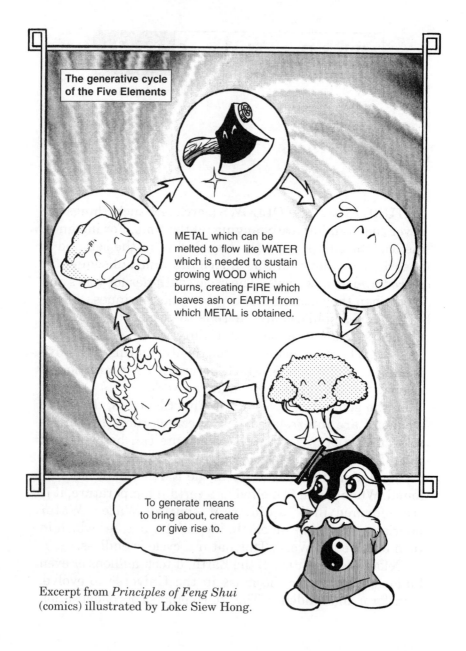

Excerpt from *Principles of Feng Shui*
(comics) illustrated by Loke Siew Hong.

went through rounds and rounds of cycle and evolution. The Earth finally condensed out of the energy such as gas and dust of the Universe. The Chinese called this energy *qi* (氣). Einstein once said, when matter is reduced to the point of invisibility, it becomes energy which means energy represents mass and vice-versa. He expressed the relationship of mass and energy as $E=MC^2$ where m is mass of the matter and c is the speed of light.

All things in Nature behave in a cyclical manner. For example, at different temperatures, water (liquid) can be transformed into ice (solid) or steam (gas). When it is in liquid form, water can be used to nourish all things and sustain life, while in solid form it can be used to preserve food. When water is in its gaseous form — steam (gas) — it expands to the point of invisibility, that is, it becomes energy. Although man uses different names to describe water, its basic elements — two atoms of hydrogen and an atom of oxygen — always remain unchanged.

Cyclical Thinking

In an organisation, it is important to design and implement effective systems as well as to cultivate "cyclical thinking" in our people. We should always treat the appraisal, reward, accounting, planning and control — just to name a few — as a system which comprises several processes. For example, an effective appraisal system comprises five processes:

(i) Setting expectations and performance goals for an employee;

(ii) Helping the employee to meet those expectations successfully;

(iii) Tracking, evaluating and reviewing performance from time to time;

(iv) Providing performance feedback and meaningful recognition and rewards;

(v) Using the actual performance as a yardstick for setting future expectations and performance goals.

In addition, we should treat the appraisal system as a sub-system to the performance system. In order to make the appraisal system effective, it is important to realistically link it to the reward system, and so on. It is also essential to review the system periodically to ensure its effectiveness; and to continuously improve or redesign all current systems and processes to position the organisation to achieve its goals.

Despite the strong emphasis placed on the development of effective systems, rules and regulations to support organisational and economy effectiveness, the fundamentals of MBO should not be overlooked. If an effective legal system can be used to manage and control human behaviour, then there will be no crimes and social problems today. Effective laws and rules are important in guiding human behaviour, but they do not make anyone more moral or ethical. It is cultural influences and good education which ultimately change, reform and shape the character of people.

It is a mistake to think that "Management By System" (MBS) — whether it is reward, disciplinary or performance management system — can be used to replace "Management By People" (MBP). In fact, if the relationship between management and employee is not well established, it will be disastrous to over-emphasise the punishment or disciplinary system. The harder you push, the harder the system will push back. We need to understand Newton's law that the reaction to an action is always equal and opposite to that action.

Consequently, it is important to balance the use of MBO and MBS for efficient management. Professional management uses MBS and "Management By Figure" to reinforce MBP and "Management By Feeling" respectively. Similarly, at the macro economic level, a country like China needs a good political and legal system for a smooth economic transition.

Life-cycle

Everything in Nature, be it plant, animal or human being, goes through a life-cycle. According to Buddhism, human beings go through a life-cycle of birth, growth, sickness and death. Similar to human beings, a product, an organisation, an industry or even an economy or the world goes through a life-cycle. It is crucial for us to understand where we are at each stage of the life-cycle and to position ourselves in order to take full advantage of it.

A man in his twenties should capitalise on his drive and be brave enough to realise his full potential. But when he reaches 45 years of age or more, he should capitalise on his life's experiences to strengthen his career. It is not an appropriate time to change career at this stage.

When a product is first launched, the producer or

manufacturer must focus on creating product awareness among his targeted customers. When the product has progressed to a growth stage, then the strategy should be to maximise the market share through developing new segments, new related products or services, and even to broaden the market geographically. Once a product has reached its maturity stage, the strategy should be to defend the market share through high advertisement levels, product improvement or product differentiation. For example, Coca-Cola has been able to maintain its product at the maturity position very well over the last few decades. Coca-Cola's life-cycle has extended beyond a century!

Not only does a product go through a life-cycle, even the brand-name or packaging also have life-cycles. Consider how the packaging of soft drinks has evolved from bottles to aluminium cans to cardboard packaging, and then to plastic containers over the years. This is the same for brands. Some brands are deemed outdated. New brands are created annually while many die out of the market.

An organisation also experiences a life-cycle. At the infant stage, the organisation is often a one-man show, surviving through low overheads with practically no established policies, systems and procedures. However, as the organisation moves to the growth stage, the emphasis is placed on organisational structure and design, the development of systems, policies and procedures, and the need for proper strategic planning, budgeting and control. If these requirements are not well established, it is difficult for the organisation to grow to the next level of advancement.

Once an organisation reaches the advanced level of growth, maintaining a balance between system and control and flexibility and creativity is essential. If the organisation fails to manage this stage properly, then there is a tendency for the organisation to be trapped in its own bureaucracy. At this bureaucratic stage, employee morale is low while turnover of good people is high; there is a decline in market share and ultimately the organisation's performance declines. If the situation is not immediately rectified, the organisation will die. Over the past two decades, many reputable and large organisations have been declared "dead" because of bureaucracy. In fact, a study has revealed that the average organisation's lifespan is only about half the human lifespan.

The Economic Cycle

All businesses go through small and big economic cycles of recession, depression, recovery and inflation. The peaks and troughs are all parts of a cycle. There is no peak without the trough.

Organisations should take the periods of economic stagnation as opportunities to rest and gather strength. It is common for many companies to cut their training budget during a recession when in fact, the reverse should be practised because it is during this time that its personnel has more time for job rotation and time to attend training courses. It is during bad times that the need for good people is even more critical. It is during this break that an organisation should focus on building up its strength and wait patiently for the next upturn. Once the opportunities present themselves, the well-prepared organisation will require little effort to materialise its dreams.

As the organisation grows from one stage to another, it is essential to take a break to consolidate its investments and financing structures by disposing part of the less

productive assets or converting unproductive assets into productive ones. Once the organisation has financially consolidated and built new strengths (better management systems and personnel qualities), then it is more ready for new heights and records. This way, the business expansion will be more stable and steady.

Whether it is for organisational development or productivity, growth always follows a "stair-case" path instead of a linear upward curve. Taking a short break during a crisis or at an appropriate time to conserve energy and build a greater reserve of energy will enable it to travel a longer journey. When a volcano has not erupted for decades, it does not necessarily mean that it will not erupt again. The inactive volcano is resting, gathering enough strength for the right timing. When it erupts, it will catch us by surprise.

The cyclical nature of the economy is also a major consideration for new businesses, new projects or new ventures. One of the basic assumptions for a business entity is a going concern which means there is no intention to liquidate it. As such, whether the business is incorporated during an inflationary or deflationary period, the business still has to face the next "up" or "down" turn. When companies increase their investments (capital or human resources) during an inflationary period, they should have in mind what they are going to do with the excess capacity during the bad times. Similarly, companies which choose to downsize their asset-base during the recession may miss out on opportunities when the economy recovers. Gains and losses are never ending cycles.

Another basic question is, "When is the best time to start a new business, project or venture?" To start a business during an inflationary period will mean a greater chance of success but the capital outlay will also be high. On the other hand, to start a business during a recessionary period, one will enjoy a low capital outlay and low operating costs, but the business' success rate will also be low. Thus, each timing has its pros and cons.

It is important to understand each stage of the economic cycle and see its opportunities. Almost every business enjoys the upward trend of the inflationary periods. But during the recessionary period, only those who are fundamentally strong, especially financially, will benefit. It is always easy to start a business — buy a real estate or invest in the stock market — but you must have the holding power and keep a long-term view of things and realise that there are always more opportunities than threats. The question is, "How can

I take advantage of the situation?"

At the macro economy level, the global economy is evolving from a resource-based to a technology-based to a knowledge-based and a service-based economy. In Southeast Asia (except Singapore), the economy is gradually moving from resource-based to one of downstream industries because of fast-disappearing natural resources. As for Hong Kong and Singapore, the trend is towards a service-based economy.

The Rotational Concept

The concept of circle is another principle of Nature that is closely related to the "Principle of Cycle". The Earth not only moves around the sun but actually rotates in its orbit. This has created day and night and the four seasons which account for the great variety of human and organisational events throughout the year.

This "rotation" or "spiralling" principle in Nature is observed particularly in the Japanese organisation where a fresh graduate is expected to begin from the lowest management level. He will then be gradually promoted to the middle management once he has been rotated among all the departments. Similarly, he needs to complete a full round of job rotation at the middle management level before being considered for the top management. The rationale is that one will not be able to make good judgement or decisions and co-ordinate well if one does not understand the activities of each individual department. In the Japanese society, personal career development focuses on "how far a person can go" instead of just "how fast a person can go".

At the organisation level, development is based on the

principle of a spiral. As the organisation develops from one stage to another, it completes a full round of activity at each stage such as developing a product, establishing a market share and building customer loyalty. At the economic level, the economy structure evolves from agriculture-based to resource-based industry before moving to hi-tech or service-based industry. At each stage of the development, an economy requires several decades to establish and consolidate its position before it is ready for the next stage of development.

To the Chinese, time is never defined as a straight line, where there is a beginning and an end. It is always defined as a circle. Time is based on the movement of the moon around the Earth and the Earth around the sun. All events go through rounds of revolutions or cycles.

This cyclical view of time also causes the Chinese businessman to view his offspring as a continuity of his life and of his wealth. To have heirs to the family's name and wealth is, to a Chinese, of primary importance if one is to be filial to one's parents. The Chinese businessman expects his wealth to be inherited by his children and grandchildren. This causes the Chinese businessman to pay special attention to the past and present while keeping an eye on the distant horizon. Similarly for an organisation, it is important to look ahead while operating in today's environment.

After centuries of pursuing material wealth, mankind today has time to smell the roses. We need good foresight as we progress so that we can take a long-term view of our lives. But while we look forward to better opportunities and a better future, we must not forget traditional wisdom. As we acquire more knowledge about things, we must not forget to read the ancient books of wisdom that we find in each of our cultures.

The Vicious Cycle

While it is important for one to cultivate cyclical thinking, one should not be trapped by, or be a victim of, one's created cycle or system. For example, war will create hatred which in turn creates more wars. This is a vicious cycle in which a cause produces an effect which in turn reinforces or becomes the cause. According to Buddhism, hatred will not remove hatred. On the contrary, one should use LOVE to dissolve hatred. Only a force opposite to itself can neutralise that force.

The vicious cycle of poverty is played out in Third World countries such as Afghanistan, Sierra Leone, Somalia, Liberia, Ethiopia, Niger and Uganda, just to name a few. Most of these countries are found on the African continent. Several decades ago, some of the Asian economies were also caught in the vicious cycle of poverty. However, over the last few decades, the dramatic social improvements and economic development have bailed many Asian countries out of the poverty cycle. What can the African countries learn from the Asian societies?

Besides effective and far-sighted leaders, Asian countries also have another thing right. They have invested heavily in educating and training their people. In Asian communities, education is viewed as an important vehicle to move upward in the social hierarchy. The Chinese society, in particular, is highly devoted to the education of their children and has invested heavily in it. In fact, education has been considered to be a wise investment that will yield the best returns and satisfaction.

Another experience that the African countries can learn from Asians is to be economically self-reliant. Over the last few decades, Asian leaders have opened up their economies to the world in terms of trade and investment. Asians believe that trade is better than aid. As an old saying goes, "Give a person a fish, he will eat for a day; teach a person how to fish, he will eat for a lifetime." It is true that certain undesirable elements may permeate their societies when their economies are open to the rest of the world, but the overall benefits of an open economy far exceed the negative effects. Deng Xiaopeng once said, "When we open our windows, there are bound to be one or two flies that will find their way into the house. But we are not going to close the window again just because of these few unwanted insects."

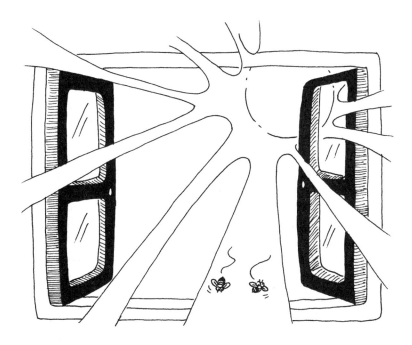

Take the case of China. Its economy has been undergoing reform — opening up its economy to the world — since 1979. But China is not going to revert to being a closed economy just because of a few negative elements as a result of opening itself to the world. This is precisely what Deng meant. China does not want to be trapped by its own communist system. If China can successfully shake off its poverty, it means one-sixth of humanity will have been lifted out of poverty. To break out of a vicious cycle, it takes courage to own up to one's mistakes and weakness in order to reinvent oneself.

In many organisations, employees are also trapped in their small vicious cycles. Day in and day out they are caught up with routine. An employee may put in a hard day's work but it will not lead him anywhere if he does not have a definite goal or aim in his work. It is important for one to work hard and be responsible towards one's organisation but one needs to have a goal in mind. Success in one's career is more than just having more money. One should have a work objective and continuously benchmark oneself against one's peers.

Doing business is like managing a mechanical system. It starts with the purchasing department procuring the right raw materials. The production department will then need to make sure that the machine is in good order to ensure that the product is of good quality. The marketing department's job is to create a demand and then fulfil it by using the right distribution and service strategies. Having a good business and cash flow are consequences of the strong coordination of all these activities. Naturally, with strong liquidity and financial positions, companies are able to purchase good materials and attract good people to join them.

But once the business is trapped in a vicious cycle, it is

extremely difficult for the company to get out of it. The purchasing department is unable to procure the right material and hence the outputs are sub-optimal which then makes marketing them extremely difficult. Without strong sales, the whole business will be trapped in liquidity and financial difficulties which will greatly handicap the company's ability to procure good materials and attract good people. A vicious cycle is perpetuated unless some dramatic remedial actions are taken to arrest the cycle.

The Perpetual Cycle

Nature always follows a never ending cycle. The cyclical nature of the Universe makes us think that the only thing constant is change. However, if we probe deeper, all changes in Nature will go back to their original states. In the broader perspective, nothing really changes. The rotating or revolving characteristics of Nature have created day and night and the four seasons. But these are a never ending cycle. What we always perceive as change in actual sense is just a matter of cycle or rotation or going round in circles.

Over the last few centuries, the study of leadership theory and effectiveness has evolved from the trait phase (1920s) to the behavioural phase (1950s) to the contingency phase (1970s). In the 1980s, management researchers began to examine the charisma of a leader in transforming an organisation. The study focuses on the qualities and characteristics of an effective leader which primarily embrace a leader's personality and behavioural attributes within a given set of environmental factors. It can be said that the development of the theory of leadership has, over the last 70 years, gone through a full cycle.

In the study of history or man's past, we see that many past human events keep repeating themselves. It is because man always takes a short-term perspective of his affairs or he has a short memory. He lacks a holistic or a long-term view of things.

The Non-rotational

In Chinese society, time has been viewed as the most valuable asset to mankind. There is a Chinese proverb that says, "An inch of gold cannot buy an inch of time"(寸金难买寸光阴), which means time is a scarce resource that once lost, will be lost forever. No one can buy time or go back to the past. Life and death are derived from the concept of time. The average human life cycle is approximately 70 to 80 years. In Buddhism, human beings are believed to go through many lifetimes through rebirths before attaining the next level of being. In this sense, every lifetime is confined to a specific time-frame.

Consider the movements of all matters in Nature: the Earth, the moon, the stars or any living organism. Notice that they all behave in a specific pattern or manner. To some extent, all movements return the body concerned to their original positions. According to Lao Zi, returning to an original position is the principle of Tao. A body returning to its original position either through a circular, rotational or spiral motion, is the way of Nature. This is the natural characteristic of Nature: all lives move in a cyclical manner.

In a timeless world, there is no beginning or end. Everything is everlasting or eternal. Life transcends time and space. Within the changing nature of all things, there lies the Tao which is independent of time and space.

The Natural Order

Not only do things move in a cyclical manner but they also follow a specific order. Flowers will have to blossom first before they can bear fruits. This natural order of event is observed at all times. In a family, it is natural for the grandfather to die first, followed by the father and then the sons. If the father dies before the grandfather, or the son dies before the father, then it is indeed a tragedy.

In the traditional Chinese society, every member of a family has a properly defined role to assume. A father is a breadwinner; a mother, a homemaker; and a child should respect the elderly. This was Confucius' prescription for harmony in a family. Confucius said, "Let the ruler be a ruler, the minister a minister, the father a father, and the son a son"(君君臣臣, 父父子子).

This natural order of rules and responsibilities should be strictly observed in an organisation or there will be conflict, confusion and frustration. If each and every individual performs his duties well and does not shirk his responsibilities, it means the natural order has been observed. What will follow is efficiency and order. Consider the consequences for an organisation if its Production personnel interfere with financial affairs, neglecting their own duties and responsibilities.

Every department should focus on its own primary functions as follows:

Production Department   - Cost efficiency with high quality of goods produced

Marketing Department   - Customer satisfaction

with high profitability

Finance Department   - Reasonable financial
risk with optimum
returns on assets and
equities

Human Resource Department - Employee satisfaction
with high labour
productivity

If every department learns to focus on its primary functions and perform them, then the organisation will prosper.

The natural order of things is also emphasised in Buddhism. The teachings of the Dharma is the core of Buddhism. According to the Dharma, one is expected to carry out and discharge his duties according to each stage of his life. Man has to follow the natural course of events and act according to the requisites of the situation. If this natural order of duty is properly carried out and followed, peace will naturally follow.

The natural order of things is applicable to all beings with no exception. So it is with the Earth itself. For millions of years, the Earth has never been free from natural disasters of earthquakes, volcanic eruptions, floods and so on. Nature is our first master. It teaches us to face life, which is always full of uncertainties and challenges.

The same principle applies to managing a business which is always full of uncertainties and competition. A business, be it at the infant, growing or maturing stage, is never free from environmental influences. An organisation is an open system which constantly interacts with the rest of the world to obtain its resources (raw material, labour and capital) and in turn sell its goods and services to society. Thus, it is essential for an organisation to continuously scan the external environment for opportunities and threats as well as the internal environment to assess its strengths and weaknesses. Organisations should learn to recognise, discover or even create organisational opportunities and be wise enough to take advantage of opportunities.

An organisation should be open and optimistic, adaptable and flexible to be able to manage environmental constraints. It should also be enthusiastic and pro-active, exploiting its strengths to the fullest, and persevering to overcome its weaknesses. Managing the environment has become the key to being successful. Knowing the environment is the first step to providing a comprehensive information network and database to plan for our future.

Summary of Learning Points

✔ Nature always follows a cycle.

✔ In an organisation, we should treat appraisals, rewards, accounting, planning and control as a system comprising several processes.

✔ "Management By People" is important to support organisational effectiveness but it should be balanced with other management tools.

✔ Everything in Nature, be it plant, animal or human being, goes through a life cycle. One should learn to manage each stage of the life cycle well.

✔ Whether one is in an inflationary or deflationary period, one needs to understand the situation and be vigilant of opportunities in that situation.

✔ The revolving characteristics of Nature has created a great variety of human and organisational events throughout the year.

✔ The cyclical view of time causes Chinese business leaders to see their offspring as an extension of themselves — a continuity of their own lives and wealth.

✔ It is important for one to cultivate "cyclical thinking" — to look for cycles in situations. But one should certainly not be trapped by one's own created cycle or system.

✔ To break out from a vicious cycle, we must be brave enough to face ourselves, admit our own mistakes and continuously challenge the status quo.

✔ Going round in a circle is in a sense being in a dead end. Nature always follows a never ending cycle.

✔ Returning to its original position either through a circular, rotational or spiral motion is the way of Nature. It is the natural characteristics of Nature whereby all lives move in a cyclical manner.

✔ In a timeless world, there is no beginning or end; everything is everlasting or eternal.

✔ Man has to follow the natural order of events closely and act according to the demands of the situation.

✔ Human nature is ever-changing and the path of life is never smooth. Just like Nature, human life is always full of uncertainties and challenges.

The Principle of Balance

EVERYTHING IN THE Universe is created for a purpose. Nothing is without its usefulness. Each existence has its place in the Universe and we must balance all these elements correctly in order to create something meaningful. About the Five Elements (Metal, Wood, Water, Fire, Earth) which we discussed in Chapter 3, we see that the Five Elements not only follow a specific order or cycle, but there also exists a link (*qi*) among them. *Qi* can be defined as the vital life force or universal energy that holds everything together. When the Five Elements are correctly balanced with *qi*, it gives rise to all natural events. This is the "Principle of Balance".

Balance is one of the characteristics of Nature. The balancing of Yin and Yang forces, the strong and the weak, man and woman, and so on, is of paramount importance in achieving universal harmony. When one side is stronger than the other, disorder, disharmony and disagreement will result. For instance, outer beauty (outer self) should be balanced with inner beauty (inner self). Similarly, if we consume too much "heaty" food (such as deep fried food), we need to balance it by taking something "cooling", otherwise we will fall sick very easily. In maintaining a healthy and balanced diet, one needs to consume a right balance of different types of food (such as balance between vegetables and meats). This is to avoid over- or under-nourishment. The ability to identify the necessary "ingredients" for a happy life is not enough for a happy life if you cannot balance them accordingly. A happy person always knows how to strike a balance between his physical, emotional, mental and spiritual needs. If a person constantly lives without his emotional needs being sufficiently met (for instance, he is deprived of love and warmth), in the long run, his physical health, intellectual capacity or even spiritual fulfilment will also be adversely affected.

Qi

Great philosophers like Lao Zi believed that Tao is the great beginning that existed before Heaven and Earth. It is Tao that created Heaven and Earth and the whole Universe. The Universe then produced the material force (*qi*) and material substances.

Qi is the life force or energy that holds everything together in the Universe. The force (gravity) that causes apples to fall to the ground is the same as the force that holds all the planets within their orbits in the solar system. Hence, force is part and parcel of everything in the Universe, which embraces all things on Earth, the rest of the planets in the solar system, the stars and the galaxies.

By its nature, a force is universal and does not have a beginning or end. It is forever evolving. Forces not only exist among all things but also within all things. For instance, an animal is said to exert more force from within than a plant does. In turn, a plant expresses more force than a rock. Among all living things, it is man that expresses the most force from within.

It is the ability to balance the mind and the body which allows one to express his or her force from within. Buddhism teaches one to achieve eternal peace, harmony and happiness through meditation. During meditation, the life force detaches from the physical body and enters into the spiritual world. According to Buddhism, it is called "Nirvana" or "Heaven". When a person dies, the life force leaves the human body and moves on to a new body to experience the next life. Hence, these forces experience numerous lifetimes or spiritual evolution.

In using the life force within us, we should seek to continuously understand, acknowledge, accept and expand it. The force within us reaffirms and reinforces whatever we are doing. Through continuous practice, we will gradually change our perception from "being the victim of the environment" to "influencing and controlling the environment". This flow of energy will be felt by others around us.

According to Buddhism, identifying the basic elements of life, balancing them and using the life force properly will set one free. The ultimate goal of living is to become a "free spirit", as Taoism teaches. The source of all misfortune comes from having a physical body. If one does not possess a body, there will be no misfortunes.

At the levels of the organisation, industry and economy, understanding the life force is of paramount importance. Without it, organisations will disintegrate, industries disappear and economies fall apart.

The Balancing Component

In an organisation, it is desirable to maintain a good balance between corporate strategy, organisational structure, operating system, technical skill and management style. If the organisation operates within a poor system and lacks the required expertees, it is unlikely that the organisation will execute its strategies well and achieve its business goals. It is also pointless to develop an advance system if there is a lack of human skills to implement it.

When an organisation develops a strategy to achieve a business goal, it must have the organisational structure, operating system, technical skills and appropriate management style to support it. These elements of success (critical success factors) account for only 50 percent of the battle; the other 50 percent comes from the ability to balance all these elements. An organisation possessing excellent business strategies and efficient operating systems will not last very long if its management style is inappropriate.

One of the main characteristics of Chinese business practices is its remarkably high degree of entrepreneurship. The extraordinary business acumen of the Chinese leader is very much shaped by Chinese cultural values, especially owing to the high value that the Chinese place on the family and glorifying the family's name. However, the Chinese entrepreneur tends to deem business management as relatively unimportant.

There is a Chinese business saying that goes like this: "It is difficult to start a new business but it is even more difficult to keep it going." (创 业 难 , 守 业 更 难) The rationale is that, to create or start a new business requires a great deal of business sense, but to maintain it calls for much management sense. In order to prolong the lifespan of a Chinese business organisation, the real challenge is to improve its management skills.

The same is also true of the West. There is a high degree of entrepreneurship in Apple Computer, for example, but the lack of a good management system for the organisation has hampered its growth. On the other hand, the strong management team in Kodak has embarked on a series of change management programmes to encourage an innovative and creative culture throughout its organisation so as to be competitive.

Today, be it the East or the West, one of the main tasks of the corporate leader is to perform a balancing act in maintaining a high degree of entrepreneurship with effective management.

The Combination

Balancing is the ability to combine the basic elements to meet the needs of a situation. If you want to produce different types of colour, you need to combine the three primary colours of red, yellow and blue in different proportions to get the colour you want.

We need to be wise in managing organisational resources. Every creation in Nature is useful. For instance, every part of a tree is useful if we know how to use it wisely. The main trunk of a tree can be used to build the pillar of the house. The main branches can be used for the doors and windows whereas the finer ones would be more suitable for making furniture and cooking utensils. The rest of the tree can be used for firewood.

From my observations, an organisation comprises people who generally fall into four categories. There are those who

are courageous and those who are timid; then there are the intelligent ones as well as the physically strong ones. Those who are courageous should be assigned challenging tasks like marketing. For those who are timid, administrative work would be suitable. The intelligent ones should be the thinkers while the physically strong ones should be the workers. All human beings have their own talents. Optimise each person's talents by assigning him the right job.

In order to have an effective management team, a combination of different types of people is essential. We need to have the good guy and the bad guy (the devil's advocate), the emotional and the analytical, as well as the young and the older ones. In short, a right balance of elements is needed for success.

The Tree Root

Keeping a good balance at the different levels in an organisational hierarchy is very important. In many business organisations, the middle management is always treated as the foundation or pillar of the organisation, just like the roots of a tree. Just as large trees need strong roots to support them, a large organisation requires strong middle management personnel. The main function of the middle management is to translate the strategic plans and objectives of the top management into operational action plans. It also serves as the medium of communication and value congruence between the upper and the lower levels of management. Middle management personnel must, above all, be good communicators, coordinators and executors of plans. Middle management should continuously balance the needs between the two levels (the level above it and the one below it) of management and achieve higher productivity through good employer-employee relationship. If the middle management is not strong in its execution of plans, the entire organisation will be jeopardised.

For example, if the middle management of an organisation does not have good and cordial relationships with the lower management, the organisation will be vulnerable to industrial conflict or human relations problem. The lower level management and staff are often sensitive and rather intolerant of mistakes committed by the top management. If the top management makes a mistake, the lower level management will take this opportunity to react negatively. When the top management takes disciplinary action, the consequence can be worse. The atmosphere will be one of "waiting to catch the management make a mistake".

Top and middle management personnel can strengthen

the "root" through greater introspection. Firstly, the management needs to learn the history of the organisation's events and evaluate its management style and practices. History is the best testimony for all management philosophy and practice. Next, it should take steps to build and enhance its relationship with the employees. Lastly, it needs to balance the needs between the top and the lower management.

When individuals or groups of individuals think, the organisation thinks. Without people, an organisation is just a building, an office or a factory. It is people who give life to an organisation. Hence, PEOPLE constitute the biggest asset of an organisation. The productivity of the machinery and equipment is governed by the "Law of Mechanics"; it is designed by the engineer. But when it comes to labour or people, it is a different matter. It can be managed. If we provide the right amount of leadership, motivation, responsibility, incentive, communication and empowerment, we are likely to get positive results. What needs to be remembered is that people themselves, to a very large extent, determine their productivity. If they are dissatisfied, they can drastically reduce their productivity. Therefore, it is important to carefully manage and stretch the abilities of the individual to the fullest. But remember that the key word is to "stretch" and not to "strain" the individual.

The Proportion

The ability to identify and balance the elements of success requires one to apply the "Principle of Proportion". It is interesting to observe the reproduction system of Nature. A small animal like a rat normally reproduces more in

numbers as compared to a large animal like an elephant. Similarly, during a particular season, a mango tree bears more fruits than in another season but the size of the mangoes are usually small.

It is essential for the management to understand and observe this Law of Proportion closely. For example, in financial management, we must balance our investment structure, ensuring that long-term investments balance with short-term investments. Similarly, in balancing our financing structure, short-term borrowing should be balanced with long-term borrowing so that we can generate enough cash surplus for re-investment or business expansion. With respect to financial leverage or capital structure, as a rule-of -thumb, total borrowing should not exceed two times that of the company's equity or shareholders' funds. However, financial leverage can be higher or lower than twice the equity depending on the type of business and its business risks. A high business risk venture should be compensated for and operated with a lower financial risk (lower financial leverage) and vice-versa.

Besides financial management, this Law of Proportion can also be applied to other aspects of management. For instance, the Pareto rule of 80:20 says that 80 percent of our performance or result comes from 20 percent of our effort. Similarly, 80 percent of our sales comes from 20 percent of our sales force; 80 percent of our problems comes from 20 percent of our activities; or 80 percent of our profit comes from 20 percent of our clients or products; and so on. During communication with a prospective customer, the listening and talking ratio should ideally be 80:20. In time management, learn to strike a balance between reactive activities and pro-active activities. Under most circumstances, it is the pro-active activities which contribute towards our performance or results.

The ability to analyse and balance things using the Law of Proportion is the most important role of our minds. We must use our common sense and discretion. The mind should have right ideas that are based on careful observations and interpret their importance correctly. Policies and procedures are formulated to handle and resolve daily matters. Under normal circumstances, it is essential to apply the normal policies and procedures to resolve an issue or solve a problem. But under unusual circumstances, if you still stick to the normal policies and procedures to handle a problem, then you are said to be incapable of using your common sense and discretion. An intelligent person knows how to think wisely and act intelligently. In action, a wise person observes correct timing.

The Different Viewpoints

According to Lao Zi, Tao is the universal principle of existence. To understand Nature is to understand Tao. To know Nature is to know Heaven. Tao began with the One. It is the One that produced the Two — Yin and Yang; and the Two produced the Three, and then thousands and millions of things. This is the nature of all existence. Although humans, animals, fish and insects are different in their nature, they all come from the great beginning. In Taoism, there is no distinction between rivers, lakes and seas as they are all just bodies of water. Similarly, it is the tree that has been transformed into houses, furniture, tools and utensils, and pulp and paper. Each has a different function, yet all come from the same source. By their true nature, they are nameless. It is man who gives them names. It is the understanding of this true nature of all existence and things that inspires one to be selfless.

The true nature of all things is subjective, as it depends on what one believes. What one believes depends on one's perception. How one perceives is only as good as one's point of view. If one has accepted a particular angle or point of view, one has to give up some other views. This is the opportunity cost. In reality, nothing is absolutely objective without embracing all viewpoints. Hence, in practice, to be able to understand and balance all viewpoints is wisdom.

The study of science is as good as human experience. Fundamentally, there is NO distinct differences between the study of science, philosophy and religion. It is just a matter of viewpoints. They all have a common objective and that is to define, describe and explain the origin of life. However, they all use a different approach.

A physicist uses a scientific approach to study Nature

and the origin of life, while a philosopher and a religionist base their studies of Nature and the origin of life on human or spiritual experiences. To many people, the study of physics deals with non-living things. This is NOT TRUE. The whole Universe is a living organism and is changing all the time. Similarly, the study of chemistry is no different from biology. The study of chemistry deals with the principle of change which is to reveal the essence or origin of life. To a physicist, there is no difference between the past and the future in explaining the principle of Nature. To Lao Zi, Tao transcends space and time. Anything that can be explained within space and time is not reality.

In defining moral values, there is no one set of criteria for right or wrong and good or bad. It depends on a given society's viewpoint. From the legal viewpoint, moral rules are no different from legal rules. What is illegal is also deemed to be immoral. If we view them as an economist, moral values are a matter of pragmatism. One person's gain is another person's loss. Before doing an unethical act, one will weigh the costs and benefits. If the benefits exceed the costs, than it is a worthwhile act to undertake. It is the ends that justify the means. From the viewpoint of Lao Zi, "good or bad" and "right or wrong" are all relative. All human events have to be described in relative terms. When we define something as right, a situation opposite to it is therefore wrong. It is not only relative to space, that is, what is morally right in one culture may be seen to be wrong in another, but also relative to time. What is morally right today may have been morally wrong one century ago.

To be able to see things from different viewpoints is an advantage. Keeping a balanced mind is one of man's greatest assets. In an organisation, a leader must not only learn to understand and accept different viewpoints, but at the same time, be able to maintain a balance between them. Management is an art of balancing.

Try to balance some of the following:

- In articulating a vision, try to balance the short-term perspective with the long-term direction.

- In planning, try to balance the present opportunities with future ones.

- In structuring, try to balance rigidity and flexibility.

- In developing strategies, try to balance internal with external variables.

- In delegating power, try to balance responsibility with authority.

- In designing a job, try to balance specialisation with job enrichment.

- In motivating people, try to balance intrinsic factors with external incentives.

- In leading people, try to balance words with deeds.

- In building team work, try to balance the number of white collar workers with the number of blue collar workers.

- In communication, try to balance words with silence.

- In controlling, try to balance the external system with

self-discipline.

* In seeking a permanent solution, try to balance short-term impacts with long-term consequences.

* In production, try to balance between quality and quantity.

The Rotational Balance

The evolution of the Earth and Nature went through processes of rotational balance. At each stage of evolution, the process goes through many rounds of rotation. At each round of rotation, a new balance is achieved. All on Earth today evolved from simple life-forms of bacteria and marine plants to gradually diversify into the current ecological system. So the evolution of life is like completing one cycle after another and trying to attain an equilibrium or a new balance at each cycle. This is how the principle of cycle is linked to the principle of balance. Again, the principle of balance is associated with the principle of change. However, all changes are achieved within the Universe. From a broad perspective, nothing has actually changed, as everything depends on everything else and everything is equal to everything else which is the Universal Whole. This is the Grand Theory of Life and Nature.

Human life is like a process. At each stage of our life cycle, we go through an experience of "not knowing what we don't know" to "knowing what we don't know". After a long period of persistence and continuous practice, we finally arrive at "not knowing what we know". For instance, a person may learn the importance of patience from his teacher. After many years of practice, patience may become part of his character when he interacts with others. It has become a natural behaviour of which he may not be aware of.

Life is a process of understanding and experiencing oneself and our surroundings. We cannot simply define life as a logical sequence of events or systems. Life is a right brain — phenomenon which is to follow the heart instead of the mind. Lao Zi always let things balance in their natural way and allowed things to unfold, based on their natural order. This is, again, a form of balancing life.

In many situations, the factor underlying the success of an individual can also be the factor which brings about his failure. It is the fin that enables a fish to swim in the water. But it is also the fin that is often trapped by the fishing net resulting in the fish being caught by the fisherman. Similarly, the wings of a bird are its greatest asset but if the wings are shot by the hunter, the bird will face the same fate as the fish.

In the marketing context, if an organisation's competitive advantage is the uniqueness of its product, then it will be vulnerable to any new product development of its competitors. In the past, many countries relied on their cheap labour costs as their main and only competitive advantage. Through the invention of very advanced machinery and better production processes, cheap labour cost is no more an absolute advantage.

The development of a good strategy entails the right combination of the basic elements of success that are in line with the environmental balance and the right timing of its implementation. In the case of marketing strategies, it is called "Marketing-Mix". This strategy mixes the four P's, namely the product strategy, pricing strategy, promotion strategy and place strategy. For example, McDonald's uses the concept of fast-food (product strategy), value-for-money (pricing strategy), heavy television advertisement (promotion strategy) and strategic location (place strategy) to develop a Marketing-Mix strategy. Competitors find it difficult to imitate or attack a mix-strategy. By combining and recombining these basic elements of the four P's, different combinations of strategies, like a kaleidoscope, will be developed.

In order to create sustainable competitive advantages, an organisation first needs to identify the critical success factors, carefully blend and balance them, and then implement them at the right time.

The Symmetry

All things in Nature come from within, including the Universe itself. The Universe is a whole which not only embraces everything but also seeks to find balance within itself. For example, when man over-exploited Nature, it reacted with a hole in the ozone layer. However, Nature has self-healing and self-balancing abilities. The hole in the ozone layer is gradually getting smaller.

For the first time in the history of mankind, the world is creating a new balance in power between Western Europe, North America and East Asia. For the past few centuries, Western Europe and North America have been economically ahead of the rest of the world. It is time for the East to match the West. Over the past two to three decades, East Asia has experienced rapid growth in its economies. The emergence of the Newly Industrialised Countries of East Asia, namely Hong Kong, Singapore, South Korea and

Taiwan followed by Indonesia, Malaysia and Thailand will provide abundant business opportunities for the world. In addition, major economic reform in China and some parts of Southeast Asia will further accelerate East Asia's economic growth. In the new world order, economic power will be the underlying factor in balancing the importance or power of the East and the West.

At the level of the economy, governments have learned many lessons and realised the importance of maintaining a balanced budgetary account and payment account. In recent years, the US government has taken dramatic measures to cut welfare expenses in pursuing a balanced fiscal budget. Similarly, many countries in Southeast Asia are also tightening their belts as a result of the currency crisis in

the late 1990s. All these point to the importance of maintaining a balanced order whether it is at the national, regional or global level.

With regard to balancing trade activities between countries, most countries today adopt neither extreme protectionism nor liberal policies. The rule for the new game is RECIPROCITY which means that two countries will seek to strike a balance between their imports and exports. If the Japanese government would like to export more goods to the United States, it should reciprocate by importing more goods from her, so that, at the end of the day, the trade flows between these two countries will be balanced.

Imperfection

Nothing in this world is perfect. It is just a matter of transition and completeness. Nature's and man's evolution will never attain "perfect perfection". It will evolve from one level of completeness to the next level. If something is said to be perfect, then it has achieved permanency, a dead end. Perfection is a form of status quo or standstill. And being still is the first step to regression. No change is a dead end while change is a sign of life. As long as something is defined to have life, it can never attain perfection. According to Lao Zi, it is impossible for one to achieve perfection in life. He himself never strove to be perfect. What he practised was NOT perfection but completeness in life. Lao Zi believed that a complete man is what is most important. If we define something as perfect, it has to be defined in relation to something else. In reality, everything exists with everything else. Nothing is absolutely dependent or independent of things around it. All things exist in interdependence.

If change is the sign of life, then balance is the essence of life. Balance is from within. At every moment, life is changing. To be able to remain in the balanced or middle state, one needs to constantly move and balance oneself. It is just like a tightrope walker who has to constantly balance himself on the rope. There is no permanent point of balance. Life is somewhat like a pendulum that swings from one end to the other. It is that central tendency that we seek; we constantly try to move to that centre as we find ourselves thrown in extreme situations.

To be able to lead a balanced life, we need to be wary of the extremes because at the extremes, everything reverts to their extremes. But to be able to experience a balanced life, one needs to experience the imbalance too. For example, to be able to truly enjoy happiness, one needs to know what is — and therefore experience — unhappiness. Too much success is as bad as too much failure. Too much of anything is always bad. Even in today's society, some rich men prefer to keep a low profile. They do not make a show of their wealth but make every effort to lead a simple life. This is another instance of balanced life.

Summary of Learning Points

✔ Each existence has its place and usefulness in the Universe.

✔ All elements in Nature need to be correctly balanced in order for something meaningful to occur.

✔ An organisation needs to keep a balance between its strategy, organisational structure, operating system, technical skill and management style.

✔ The Law of Proportion teaches us that all elements in the Universe balance themselves naturally.

✔ An individual's productivity depends on the right amount of leadership, motivation, responsibility, incentive, communication and empowerment.

✔ The ability to analyse and balance things using the Law of Proportion is the mind's most critical role.

✔ The factor underlying the success of an individual can also be the factor behind his failure.

✔ An organisation should develop many competitive advantages and then weld them together, so that the competitors will find it difficult to imitate or attack the mix-strategy.

✔ The true nature of all things is subjective, as it depends on what one believes.

✔ To be able to see things from different viewpoints is an advantage. Keeping a balanced mind is one of man's greatest assets.

✔ At each round of rotation, a new balance or equilibrium will be achieved.

✔ Nature has self-healing and self-balancing ability.

✔ The rule for the new game in global trade is RECIPROCITY.

✔ Perfection is a form of status quo or standstill where there will no longer be change. Change is a sign of life while balance is an essence of life.

✔ Leading a balanced life is more important than attaining perfection.

The Principle of Change

THE UNIVERSE IS not static. It is changing all the time. Everything (human beings, animals, trees or even stones and rocks) in Nature is a living thing. Change is the basic principle of Nature. It is only a matter of how fast that change is for us to perceive. For example, a stone could take hundreds of years to change. It changes but its rate of change is so slow, we do not perceive it as changing.

In relation to the Principle of Change, let us consider one of the most powerful yet mystical books in the human evolution of ancient China, the *I-Ching* (*Book of Changes*). Although it is difficult to trace the exact time of its origin, its discovery has been claimed to be about 6,000 years ago. History has revealed that many rulers and Chinese philosophers have read and used the *I-Ching* for guidance.

The *I-Ching* is a sociological study for all natural events. The observation and analysis of the workings of the Universe are then conceptualised into sets of hexagrams. Based on the technique of binary system (the Yin and the Yang principle), 64 (two to the power of six) hexagrams of different patterns are formed. Each of the 64 hexagrams represents a separate scenario or situation but when all the 64 scenarios are studied collectively, all major natural and human events are represented.

115

All natural and human events undergo a series or process of change. In the *I-Ching*, change can be briefly classified into three categories, namely sequential, non-sequential and consequential changes. A sequential change is also known as cyclical change such as day and night and the four seasons. A non-sequential change is represented by long swings of cycles such as life-cycles of living things. Consequential change is the result of cause and effect. All events have their cause and consequence. Although a consequential change does not follow any specific cycle of pattern, change always takes the path of least resistance. Besides categorising the different types of change, one can also classify change: fast, slow, stop or reverse.

In the earlier chapters, from the doctrine of Yin and Yang which is emblematic of the universal unity to cyclical and sequential evolution of all things, all elements need to be correctly balanced in order to create something meaningful. Yin and Yang, the two sides of the same coin, embrace the universal oneness. Both are parts of the whole. The interaction of Yin and Yang gives rise to all natural events such as day and night and the four seasons. When Yin and Yang are properly balanced and maintained, the cyclical nature of events will last and hence change is a natural process. This also explains why all things and events undergo change or transformation in a specific order and are subject to cyclical or circular motion. The whole Universe is in an endless process of change. This principle of change works in Nature and is also applicable to human and organisational events.

Change is a natural event. A snake has to shed its old skin to allow growth and change to take place. One should continuously study the pattern of change, that is, the speed and the direction of the change. It is a great challenge to cope with a high speed of change combined with diverse directional change. Such rapid change is called "quantum" or "turbulent" change.

Change can either be reactive or pro-active. If we follow market directions closely (Market Driven), we are exhibiting reactive change. Alternatively, we can lead the market or customer by developing new products (Market Driving) and be pro-active in bringing about change. As an organisation grows from one stage to another, it is essential to make necessary changes in order to grow. Sometimes, you have to break with the past and cast away all the old ways of doing things or old habits in order to enter a new stage of the life-cycle. Nobody knows when a quantum change may be necessary, but we must always be prepared.

The Least Resistance

When water flows from the mountain to the river, it naturally follows the course of least resistance. So do human beings and organisations. The success of an individual depends on how well he can harmonise his aims and values

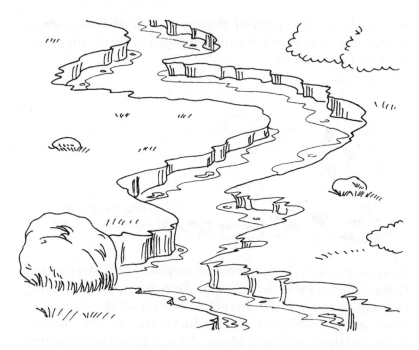

with that of his community's. The simplest path to achieve an individual's objective is to understand and follow the path of least resistance.

In an organisation, change will also take place along the path of least resistance. In order to successfully initiate change, an organisation should seek the penetrating points. For example, if among all departments, the personnel in the Finance Department are most receptive to change, then let the Finance Department be the penetrating point. Change efforts initiated in the Finance Department first will gain the confidence of all personnel when successes are noticed. Similarly, in a conglomerate, top management should carefully choose one or two of its more receptive companies to pilot new change programmes before moving on to full-scale implementation.

One of the main ingredients of success is the ability to correctly identify the path of least resistance and make success a natural event.

The Right Leverage

Successful organisational change programmes need not be huge programmes. Very often, small change programmes can lead to major work improvement. Looking for the right leverage is the effective way to implementing change.

In most organisations, the overall poor performance is often not due to poor methodology or system. More often than not, it is because of the organisation's leader. As the Chinese saying goes, "To capture a snake, catch the portion just below the snake's head." (打 蛇 打 七 寸) In a Chinese organisation, we go to the person just below the owner, that is the Managing Director or the General Manager.

When a functional division is not performing well, it reflects badly on the Managing Director or General Manager. It is the responsibility of top management personnel to manage the performance of each functional division. In the last two decades, the poor performance of several large US multinationals was arrested after the Chief Executive Officer (CEO) was replaced.

The Change Leader

For any successful organisational change to be sustained, it should be initiated and fully supported from the top. Once the organisational leader has taken the first step of change,

all the change efforts at the middle management level will be easily followed by the lower level. Just like a fish swimming — once the head has turned, the body will find it easy to turn and the tail will follow.

Research has revealed that charismatic leadership is a powerful force in reforming or transforming an organisation into a dynamic movement. A charismatic leader who is recognised and accepted by his subordinates strongly facilitates the transformation process.

A good leader is charismatic, intelligent, motivating, forward looking and has a high sense of achievement and self-confidence. A charismatic leader pays special attention to the past and the present while keeping an eye on the long-term horizon. The ability to view the future is critical in providing the organisation with a broad perspective.

With regard to intellectual capacity, a charismatic leader possesses several qualities such as good judgement and prediction, strong photographic memory, and the ability to grasp ideas and process information quickly. These qualities have been known to create a record of extraordinary accomplishments.

In motivating his staff, a charismatic leader does not rely solely on extrinsic factors such as monetary and non-monetary benefits. Instead, a change leader uses more psychological influence and emotional appeal to motivate his followers. A leader provides appropriate role-modelling; he walks his talk.

A high sense of achievement is the primary motivating force behind a change leader. He works hard and continuously communicates high expectations to his followers. Such a leader is confident that given the right synergy, anything is possible. Success would be but a matter of picking the right time.

The Change Process

A change leader is a navigator who provides direction. Once the change direction has been fixed, all efforts should be channelled towards it. In all directional change, the speed of change has to be carefully studied. The speed of change should be gradual otherwise the large ship that is being steered in a new direction may just overturn. Similarly, in changing an organisation or even a country, the speed of change should be closely monitored. As seen in the history of mankind, large economies had suffered bloodshed when change came too suddenly and too fast.

The biggest challenge of all change efforts is overcoming the resistance from the people and managing the transition process. In general, people do not resist change — they only resist being changed. Once change is imposed, resistance is always strong.

In all organisational change, human resistance is unavoidable. Some of the major causes of resistance are old habits, "loss of face", lack of motivation and faith, and uncertainty of the future. The old ways of doing things and the old paradigms are always more comfortable. When comfort sets into thinking and behaviour, it is difficult to create change. It takes tremendous effort and time to create awareness and change thought patterns before behavioural change can follow. In many cases, the management feels very proud about its past successes and is reluctant to admit current problems and weaknesses. It will be a "loss of face", as well as a challenge to the ego and status, to admit its weaknesses.

"We have tried it before but it was not successful" or "It is not going to work here", are some common remarks made when change is suggested. People become prisoners of their own past mistakes and experiences. Their negative thinking and scepticism have led to a lack of motivation and faith to see through the whole change effort. In some cases, people are sceptical and uncertain about the future. They lack confidence that things will be better after the change.

In managing the transition process, change leaders require self discipline and commitment to the original plan. Perseverance and single-mindedness are critical elements of success. Plan the work and work the plan. Create small and interrelated successes to motivate people. Very often, the change leader moves forward and then backward as a strategy. There is a Chinese war strategy that says, "We retreat in order to advance, and we advance in order to retreat."(以退为进, 以进为退).

In today's management, there is a need to continuously diagnose and renew an organisation. However, in seeking change, the change leader must possess a strong sense of the past and remember to keep at least a shadow of the organisation's traditions.

The Flip Side

Many people perceive change and crises negatively. In reality, change and crises present invaluable opportunities. According to a Chinese saying, "It is the environment that creates a truly great leader and not the other way round." (时势造英雄而非英雄造时势) When a major change takes place (such as a technological breakthrough), thousands of opportunities are created. Similarly, during a crisis (such as an earthquake or a political revolution), new industries are born. When the British and Dutch made colonies of Southeast Asian countries to exploit their rich resources, the local people saw it as a threat whereas the Chinese immigrants capitalised on it. Not only did they jump at the opportunities that emerged, but they also created opportunities for others in doing so.

An employer should provide opportunities that allow staff to do what they are best at and thus help make achieving excellence a natural event. Opportunities should be created not only for employees, but for suppliers, bankers and consumers as well. New opportunities for joint-venture or partnership, for example, with our suppliers, will not only ensure continuous supplies of materials, but also serve as an entry barrier to newcomers into the industry. Similarly, bankers can be made shareholders by offering them share options. In so doing, the financial risk (risk of liquidation) of the business can be minimised.

Instead of treating customers as "targets", make them a source of market intelligence by continuously obtaining feedback and information from them. It is our customers who have access to first-hand information about our competitor's strategies and products. If we can provide enough opportunities for our employees, suppliers, bankers and customers to be on our side, then our only opponent is our competitors. In such sense, the winning ratio is 5:1 and our success rate is very much enhanced.

The Space-time

All changes and creations only exist within space and time. But to Lao Zi, Tao transcends space and time. Although there is no precise definition for space and time, physicists like Einstein believe that space and time are interrelated. According to some calculations, the speed of light is 186,000 miles per second. As light takes time to travel, we can possibly see the past. Those stars that we can observe in the sky are actually a few millions light-years away. Logically speaking, they are the past. Based on this phenomenon, if one can travel faster than light, one can actually go back to the past. However, up to this day, scientists have yet to find anything that can travel faster than light. Using the space-time analogy, change is only relevant within space and time. Beyond that, nothing can be defined.

In the context of human and organisational events, we normally measure change across space (that is between one man and another, between one company and another, between one country and another) and time (between past and present). It is common for one company to benchmark its strategy, structure, product, work process and overall performance against different competitors, that is, make comparisons in these areas over space. Besides, companies also make such comparisons over time or longitudinally.

At the level of an economy, it is also common to use National Income or Gross National Product (GNP) statistics to compare the standards of living enjoyed by people of different countries. Comparisons can also be made of standards of living enjoyed by people of the same country over different time periods.

The Quantum Leap Change

Most of the inventions in the world came about with a quantum leap in the thinking of man. For example, when Thomas Edison invented the light bulb, his intention was not to improve the kerosene lamp. It was a quantum leap in his thinking — a very adventurous and far-sighted vision on his part — and a new paradigm.

The Japanese has learned much from the Americans for the past half a century. The Kaizen Management concept of the Japanese was developed based on the Demming Theory from the West. This management concept teaches us to make continuous improvement in the ways we get things done. In fact, the Japanese have popularised and benefited a lot from the practice of Kaizen Management. But in today's fast-moving societies, continuous improvement is not enough. Not only is change no more at a constant speed, it is increasing at an exponential rate. What the Americans are currently doing is to create a breakthrough or quantum leap in the ways they get things done. This is what we call "Business Re-engineering".

Business Re-engineering is a technique to radically improve performance by challenging and redesigning the core business and its processes using operational, technical and business knowledge in a collective manner. The assumptions on which the organisation had been built one to two decades ago will soon no longer fit in the current situation. The way we assume the external environment such as the society structure, the market, the customer and the technology are different from two to three decades ago. Besides, we must create a self-generating organisation structure that will allow the organisation to continuously re-invent itself for excellence.

In today's organisation, we talk more about culture and network, team and effective communication rather than about discipline and control. Most value-added activities in the organisation are moving from manual to intellectual ones. We now emphasise "quality people" over mere number of staff. The focus of change should be more people-oriented than system-oriented.

The Unchanged

While many management writers talk about the necessity and the benefits of change, it is also important to understand and appreciate consistency. Just as Nature changes from moment to moment, there are, however, certain things or principles in Nature which remain unchanged throughout all changes. Imagine what would happen if the Earth's gravity varies from moment to moment.

Although the world's economic activity has gone through tremendous changes over the last half century, business theories and Western management concepts only change gradually. The theories of business and management normally change slowly and gradually although business and management techniques and practices change at a faster rate.

Understanding changes is important but understanding the principles behind them is even more essential although more difficult. In an organisation, the accounting records and figures change from moment to moment but the accounting concept and principle behind the figures remain relatively constant and consistent. Otherwise, there will be no basis to compare those figures over a period of time. See how important it is to keep the accounting principle relatively consistent?

Change is a natural process but don't force change for the sake of changing. Constantly try to understand and learn from the process of change and the principle behind all that remain unchanged.

The Creative

In many organisations, creativity is treated as a rare commodity or resource, a gift or an inborn talent. This perception is not true. In managing an organisation today, the ability to create has become a MUST and not an additional competency or advantage. Organisations need to be creative in order to survive.

Creativity is most important in problem-solving and generating alternatives that are both functional and innovative. In the process of generating alternatives, both deductive and inductive thinking should be used. Deductive thinking is the ability to properly define a problem and then seek different ways to solve it. Inductive thinking, on the other hand, is to recognise a powerful idea and then look for problems that can possibly be solved by this idea.

Change and creativity are closely linked. Both are equally important for organisational success and survival. Organisations should be creative and constantly adopt different angles of defining their business and problems. Otherwise, we will be constantly trapped by our own old perceptions or old paradigms. A fish will only know it had been living in a goldfish bowl if it gets out of the goldfish bowl. Likewise we should avoid sinking into "safe" zones but wake up and be brave enough to step out of our comfort zones. We need to be courageous and continuously challenge ourselves.

The Creative Force

To apply the Principle of Change we must seek first to understand the forces of Nature. A force in Nature is invisible, like the force of gravity, but its impact is tremendous. The Earth, the solar system and the entire Universe are shaped by the forces of Nature. Over the last few hundreds of years, mankind has made great efforts to understand and learn from the forces of Nature.

If the forces of Nature are properly managed, they will greatly benefit mankind. For example, water currents can generate electricity to support industries. If we channel water into a narrow pipe, it can generate energy used for turning a turbine.

As human beings, who are part of Nature, we naturally

inherit natural forces within us. It is important to understand these forces within us and learn to effectively use them for meaningful purposes. In Sun Tzu's *Art of War*, it is stated:

"Knowing one self and knowing others will lead to 100 percent success."
知彼知己者，百战不殆。

"Knowing one self but not knowing others will lead to 50 percent success."
不知彼而知己，一胜一负。

"Not knowing one self and not knowing others will lead to 100 percent failure."
不知彼，不知己，每战必殆。

Excerpt from *Sunzi's Art of War* (comics) illustrated by Wang Xuanming.

Thus, knowing both oneself and others gives us the power to succeed.

In an organisation, capital and human resources can be considered as forces or forms of energy. These forces can be channelled into productive energy and yield results. With the right combination of resources (natural, human and capital), organisational performance will be optimal.

Creativity

If you have some free time, spare a few minutes to look at a flower — you will realise how wondrous Nature is. Its creation is so beautiful and complete. No matter how intelligent man is, it is unlikely that man's creations can ever match Nature's handiwork. Birds, reptiles and insects come from eggs. Chickens are hatched from eggs. An egg, as we know, consists of a yolk and the egg white. When a bird hatches from an egg, numerous transformations take place and ultimately a chick breaks out of the shell. The whole process from a simple element of "yolk and white" to a chick is a MIRACLE.

In today's fast-changing society, we all believe that creativity is essential. But it is difficult to provide a meaningful definition for the word "creativity". In a strict sense, the meaning of creativity only exists in the mind. Different people will define creativity differently. Some may associate creativity with originality. However, no human creation is totally original. It is because our thoughts are, in one way or another, influenced by our past readings or someone else's thoughts.

In the organisational context, there is a difference

between an effective and efficient person. Effectiveness can be defined as "doing the right things" while efficiency can be defined as "doing things right". There is also a difference between a leader and a manager. A leader is said to be effective when he performs the job well through creativity. On the other hand, an efficient manager merely follows what has been laid down by the leader. To compete well and excel in today's competitive business environment, we need more leaders (creative people) than managers (obedient people).

Although there is NO magic formula or equation that can bring about creativity in a person, there are some general principles which might stimulate creativity in us. These general principles are as follows:

- Develop greater awareness of the surroundings and consciously seek to see things from different angles (be insightful).

- Study the pattern and relationship of events and try to make sense of them by relating one to the other.

- Learn to maintain the balance of all viewpoints.

- Use plenty of imagination and both the right and left hemisphere of the brain to generate new ideas.

- As change is no more of the form of a linear equation, we must learn to see things "cross-sectionally".

- Study and understand Nature and the laws of Nature closely and use them as a source of inspiration.

- Always keep the whole picture and maintain holistic

thinking.

• Develop an action plan for our thoughts.

The spirit of creativity and innovation is seen in trying out new ideas. In order to have a good idea, we must first explore lots of ideas. The best way to learn to be innovative is to learn constantly. This is what we call learning through learning.

Man learns through making mistakes. A leader should stand behind an organisational culture that encourages his employees to take initiative and be creative. Only in this way can employees grow with the business. To tell his employees that the organisation's culture must be a "NO MISTAKE" culture would be disastrous. It not only kills initiative but the confidence and morale of employees as well. A person who makes no mistakes also does nothing worthwhile. Although making mistakes may be expensive to the business, in the long run the benefits exceed the costs. It is all right if employees make mistakes — as long as they do not repeat them. An employee who repeats his mistakes has not learned from his earlier errors. Such a behaviour should be strictly discouraged. Making mistakes is part and parcel of the learning process. Good judgement comes from experience while experience comes from making poor judgement.

The Imagination

Our day-to-day activity is very much governed by our conscious mind which is logical, rational and analytical. When we are asleep, dreams are a result of our subconscious mind at work, which we are not wholly aware of when we are awake. The difference that lies between reality and dreams is imagination. Imagination is the interaction between the conscious and subconscious mind in which the mind is in a state of relaxation especially during daydreaming. It is a state of relaxed alertness that facilitates inspirational thinking. According to Einstein, some of his major scientific discoveries grew out of his imagination rather than from analytical thinking and reasoning. Once he had an idea from his imagination, he would then use the left hemisphere of his brain to analyse it.

To be able to imagine or visualise, we must first learn to release our negative thoughts, keep a tranquil mind, relax our bodies and gradually divert our energies into positive thoughts and actions. This will then develop into deep concentration which will heighten creativity.

Imagination is the first step towards creativity. Often, in the beginning, an idea may sound utterly ridiculous. But things that were once deemed ridiculous or impossible in the past, make absolute sense today. For example, a few centuries ago, if you told someone that man would one day travel in the air (that is, fly), they would probably have thought that you were talking nonsense. But today, it is a reality.

Many of men's inventions were inspired by Nature. The idea of the refrigerator was born when its inventor visited the Arctic. The aeroplane and computer are man's attempts at replicating the bird's wing and human brain respectively. Nature is a good source of idea generation. Use the principle of Nature to help you get a good idea. What works well in Nature for millions of years should, logically, work well for man. According to Einstein, imagination is more important than knowledge. Understanding the laws of Nature is the

greatest achievement of mankind.

The Human Trap

Man creates many things for his convenience. However, very often, man is trapped by his own creations. For example, money was created as a medium of exchange but today many people are trapped by their greed for more of it. In pursuing money, the true meaning of life is often forgotten.

Similarly, man created organisations to tap resources — natural, capital and human. But people today do not appear to enjoy as much freedom as people in the past. In the old days, people decided when to start work and when to end their day at work. There were no strict rules, regulations or procedures to obey and follow.

However, despite their many trappings and limitations, many things that man has created are beneficial. The quality of material life that we enjoy today is the fruitful outcome of man's creativity. Still, if we look around the world, there are many organisations and countries that are very poorly managed. Each year, millions of valuable resources are wasted because of poor management. It is because of this rapid depletion of natural resources around the world that good management skills are ever so important.

The Logical

Reasoning is based on logical thinking. When a scientist attempts to understand Nature, he is actually using his logical thinking and reasoning powers. Logic is a left brain phenomenon. Can Nature only be understood using logical thinking? What about those lower beings which do not possess logic? Can they also perceive Nature in their own ways? Using logical and rational thinking will enable us to make sense of relationships among things. But we cannot be sure if Nature or reality can only be perceived and understood using logic or rational thinking alone.

In observing and comparing the East and the West, there is an inclination for the Westerner to perceive in a more logical or rational manner than the Easterner. In describing Nature, the Easterner tends to use a metaphysical approach based on intuition. It is perhaps for this reason that the Easterner is sometimes described as superstitious.

According to the *I-Ching*, change follows certain logic which can be broadly categorised into sequential or cyclical and consequential or causal. However, the *I-Ching* also classifies change as non-sequential, which means that it is a change that does not follow any pattern. Something is said to be logical if it can be explained with reason. But in life, there are lots of things that cannot be logically explained or understood. That is why the ultimate cause of all things is always kept unknown. Such questions as *how*, *when* and *from where* the great beginning came about have remained unanswered. If there is such a thing as space, then what is outside space? If there is such a thing as time, then what was before the beginning of time? Hence, according to Lao Zi, the ultimate truth has to transcend space and time. "Spacelessness" — the absence of space — is beyond boundary while timelessness means eternity. To him, anything that can be explained within space and time is only superficial reality. The ultimate reality is beyond logic and rationalisation.

Since life is full of uncertainties, there is no such thing as a certain answer to all questions. Knowing a thing itself is subjective. In order to live in this unexplained and uncertain world, one needs to embrace all things, including life and death, being and non-being, existence and non-existence, space and "spacelessness", time and timelessness, and so on. Understand and accept all things and maintain the universal oneness, then space and time will not exist.

The New Reality

Eastern philosophy emphasises the cultivation of the inner self and it is from the realisation of the inner self that the ultimate truth will be revealed (the "inside-out" approach). In contrast to the meditation approach, Western science uses experiments to explore and discover Nature (the "outside-in" approach). However, the Tao teaching stipulates that whatever discovery that can be described with language, symbol or any form of thought is a superficial reality of Nature. Even if we combined Eastern ancient wisdom with Western modern science, it may still be inadequate to describe the physical world. Unifying all existing concepts over space and time, it still will not reveal a unified whole. This is because reality goes beyond space and time, according to Taoism.

No existing principle or concept can accurately explain everything. It is nothing more than our minds producing figments of imagination There is no single reality that can possibly describe and explain all existence. Physicists, philosophers and religionists are merely creating their own language to explain their mental image of the reality. They are said to be very good at understanding Nature. Whether we use Western science or Eastern philosophy to describe Nature, reality is beyond being and non-being, existence and non-existence, and space and time. It is better for us to live without knowing than to provide a wrong answer. Moreover, it is not wrong to live without knowing the meaning and origin of life.

The future of mankind lies in the ability to marry Eastern philosophy with Western modern science to create breakthroughs in the exploration and understanding of the origin of life and the whole Universe. It will require a massive shift in our paradigm, our frame of thought, which I call "transformational". This is the great challenge that lies before man. One step towards effectively managing this transformation process is the ability to deal with contradiction and uncertainty. We have to continuously re-look the way we think and re-think the way we look at things.

Summary of Learning Points

✔ Everything in Nature has life — therefore everything is constantly changing and is changeable.

✔ Change is a natural event. Nothing is constant or keeps its status quo.

✔ Quantum or turbulent change is change of great speed involving diverse directions.

✔ Change always follows the path of least resistance. In order to successfully initiate change, an organisation should determine the penetrating point which is the point of least resistance.

✔ A minor or small change may lead to a major change. The small change provides the leverage for the greater change.

✔ Changing the organisational leader may lead to an improvement in the organisation's performance because, very often, the organisation's problems lie with its leader.

✔ Change and crises are the main sources of opportunities. According to a Chinese saying, "It is the environment that creates a truly great leader and not the other way round."

✔ Not only is change taking place at a non-constant speed, it is increasing at an exponential rate.

✔ Business Re-engineering is a technique to radically improve performance by challenging and redesigning the core business and its processes using operational, technical and business knowledge at the same time.

✔ Despite the constant changes of Nature, there are certain things or principles which will always remain unchanged.

✔ The ability to create is the essence of Nature.

✔ No matter how intelligent man is, it is unlikely that man's creations can ever match Nature's handiwork.

✔ No human creation is totally original.

✔ For a leader to tell the organisation's employees that he stands for a "NO MISTAKE" culture would be disastrous. Making mistakes is part of the learning process.

✔ Imagination is the interaction between the conscious and subconscious mind when the mind is in a state of relaxation.

✔ Imagination is the first step towards creativity. According to Einstein, imagination is more important than knowledge.

✔ The forces in Nature are invisible yet powerful. If natural forces are properly managed, they will greatly benefit the development of mankind.

✔ Man has created many things for his own benefit but his creations often become his own trappings. It is better for us to live without knowing a thing than to have a wrong answer.

✔ Reasoning is based on logical thinking. But we cannot be sure if Nature can only be perceived and understood by using logical and rational thinking alone.

✔ Anything that can be explained within space and time is only superficial reality.

✔ The ultimate reality transcends space and time. The ultimate reality is beyond logic and rationalisation.

✔ Reality goes beyond space and time. The ultimate reality is beyond being and non-being, existence and non-existence.

Conclusion

The study of Nature cannot be exhausted and perhaps sometimes leaves us with more questions than answers. In studying Nature, a Chinese uses more of a metaphysical approach than a scientific methodology. This metaphysical approach of studying Nature is based not on detailed observation of the natural features of the world which would be a pure science approach, but on the cultivation of the self through deep concentration of the mind. It is through continuous study of the human nature that the principles of Nature will be revealed. To a Taoist, the cycle of birth and death teaches us that everything comes from Nature and goes back to Nature.

According to Taoism, man having evolved from Nature, should continuously seek to understand, learn and live in harmony with the principles and laws of Nature. Should we continue to fight with each other and exploit Nature, it is only a matter of time that the Earth will no longer be home to man.

The ultimate answer to all human problems is understanding one's self and understanding life. The understanding of the way of life comes from self-understanding, self-introspection, self-preservation and self-cultivation. Nothing can be more meaningful and worthwhile than understanding self and life and living harmoniously with Nature. Consequently, to destroy Nature is to destroy man. Accept all things in Nature but do not become attached to anything. Live in accordance with the principles of Nature and we will find ourselves free — free of the grip of anything on Earth.

Human nature is ever-changing and the path of life is

always full of uncertainties. Nothing in the world is permanent — everything is changing and unpredictable. In reality, there is no absolute good or bad about the things in the world. It depends entirely on how one looks at them. What is true and right today may be untrue and wrong the next day. If man can grasp the essence of this principle of life, then there is no difference between a raindrop and the ocean. Man has to learn to follow the natural course closely and act according to the situation.

Both life and death arise from the mind and exist within the mind. The human mind is the master of all events and all situations. In the teachings of Buddha, a wise person chooses to purify the mind by eliminating the five evils of his mind, which are egoism, greed, anger, foolishness and fear, through the practice of personal endurance. All things are primarily controlled, ruled and created in the mind. It is through the practice of mind control that one is able to enjoy inner peace.

The source of these five evils of the mind can be briefly described in the following way. People become egotistical when they cannot detach themselves from fame and success. They become greedy as a result of having wrong ideas about satisfaction whereas anger is felt when one is being overpowered by one's passions. A person acts foolishly when he is unable to judge right from wrong. When a person experiences fear, it is because he is unwilling to face the risk of failure. In reality, most of our fears are a thousand times more than the risks and they are often unfounded. Fear, like egoism, greed, anger and foolishness, is only a state of the mind and is the main obstacle to a person's growth.

When one is unable to eliminate these five evils from the mind, others will use them to generate evil behaviours.

Through self-cultivation and introspection, one is protected from the evil thoughts of others.

To continuously understand one's self allows one to understand others better. In fact, the best way to reveal the weaknesses of others is to continuously understand one's self. Once you deeply understand yourself, the weaknesses of others will be revealed. A person who wants to conquer others must first be able to conquer his own mind.

Over the last few thousands of years, man has gone through many rounds of evolutionary change. Nature itself continuously undergoes the cycle of creation and destruction. It also has the ability to create and to "destroy". To create is to destroy and vice-versa. Birth is the beginning of death and death is the beginning of birth. Although destruction is natural and inevitable, it must be part of the natural process. Never create destruction too fast and too soon through the development of a new product, new market, new technology, new territory and so on. Manage it carefully and wait for the right time.

Birth and death are part and parcel of a cycle and the transformation process. We should continuously treat "birth and death", "new and old", "good and bad", "right and wrong", "male and female", "day and night", "east and west", and so on, each as one concept. Develop this holistic thinking. Or else, the world will never achieve eternal peace.

It is the human mind, which processes the ability to think, that gives life a meaning. The way we perceive and understand things around us all happens in the mind. Beyond that, the reality of nothing can be explained. The ultimate explanation for all things are not always fully understood. Ultimately, all things belong to the UNIVERSAL ONENESS, with no disparity or distinction... this is the Universal Principle.

Bibliography

1   Bob, Messing, *The Tao of Management*, Wildwood House, England, 1989.

2   Bond, H. M. and Hwang, Kwong-kuo, *The Social Psychology of Chinese People*, edited by Michael Harris Bond, Oxford, Hong Kong, 1986.

3   Brash, Graham, *The Saying of Confucius*, National Printers Ltd., Singapore, 1983.

4   Bukkyo, Dendo Kyokai, *The Teaching of Buddha*, Toppan Printing Co. (S) Pte. Ltd., Singapore, 1966.

5   Capra, Fritjof, *The Tao of Physics*, Harper Collins Publishers, London, 1976.

6   Chen, Jingpan, *Confucius as a Teacher*, Delta Publishing Sdn. Bhd., Malaysia, 1990.

7   De Bary, William Theodore, *Sources of Chinese Tradition*, Columbia University Press, New York and London, 1960.

8   Diane, Dreher, *The Tao of Personal Leadership*, Harper Collins Publishers, USA, 1996.

9   Drucker, Peter F., *The Frontiers of Management*, William Heinemann Ltd., London, 1986.

10   Drucker, Peter F., *The New Realities*, Heinemann Professional Publishing Ltd., 1989.

11   Drucker, Peter F., *Managing for the Future*, Butterworth Heinemann, 1992.

12   Drucker, Peter F., *Post-Capitalist Society*, Butterworth Heinemann, 1993.

13   Drucker, Peter F., *Managing in a Time of Great Change*, Butterworth Heinemann, 1995.

14   Edelman, Joel and Mary Beth Crain, *The Tao of Negotiation*, Harper Collins Publishers, 1993.

15   Fung, Yu-Lan, *A Short History of Chinese Philosophy*, The Free Press, New York, 1948.

16   Grigg, Ray, *The Tao of Relationships*, Wildwood House, England, 1989.

17   Grigg, Ray, *The Tao of Being*, Wildwood House, England, 1990.

18   Handy, Charles, *The Age of Unreason*, Business Books Ltd., London, 1989.

19   Hazel, Peter, *Ancient Chinese I Ching*, Pelanduk Publications, Malaysia, 1990.

20   Heider, John, *The Tao of Leadership*, Wildwood House, 1990.

21 Herman, M. Standley, *The Tao at Work*, Jossey-Bass Publisher, San Francisco, 1994.

22 Hu, C.N., *Zen: Key to Your Undiscovered Happiness*, Eastern Dragon Books, 1992.

23 Krause, G. Donald, *The Way of the Leader*, The Berkley Publishing Group, New York, 1997.

24 Lau, D.C., *Lao Tzu: Tao Te Ching*, Penguin Group, 1963.

25 Liang, Congjie, *The Great Thoughts of China*, John Wiley and Sons, 1996.

26 Lin, Yutang, *My Country and My People*, William Heinemann Ltd., London, 1939.

27 Lip, Evelyn, *36 Chinese Tactics for Success*, Shing Lee Publishers Pte. Ltd., Singapore, 1991.

28 Loke, Siew Hong, *Principles of Feng Shui*, Asiapac Books, Singapore, 1998.

29 Porter, Michael E., *The Competitive Advantage of Nations*, New York Press, 1990.

30 Seow, Jeffrey, *The Complete Analects of Confucius Vol 1-3*, Asiapac Books, Singapore, 1997-98.

31 Sheh, Seow Wah, *Chinese Management*, MPH Distributors Sdn. Bhd., Malaysia, 1995.

32   Tom, Peter, *Liberation Management*, Ballantine Books, New York, 1992.

33   Wang, Xuanming, *Sunzi's Art of War*, Asiapac Books, Singapore, 1998.

34   Wang, Xuanming, *Thirty-six Stratagems*, Asiapac Books, Singapore, 1998.

35   Yi, Cheng, *I Ching: The Tao of Organization*, Eastern Dragons Books, Malaysia, 1991.

LIVING 21 SERIES

Timeless Wisdom from Chinese Classics

**Timeless principles to help you achieve personal and team goals,
exploit new opportunities and define your cutting edge,
and stay on top of the changes in the next millennium.**
(A5, 136-144pp, B/W comics)

Enjoy 10% discount and free postage.

Title	Qty	*Price S$	Total
The Chinese A.R.T. of Goal Setting		$9.73	
The Chinese T.A.C.T.I.C. in Negotiation		$9.73	
The Chinese Art of Leadership		$9.73	
The Chinese Art of Excellence		$9.73	

Prices indicated after 10% discount (GST inclusive)
Offer is for readers in Singapore only.

I wish to purchase the above-mentioned titles at the nett price of S$ _____

Enclosed is my postal order/money order/cheque/ for S$_____ (No.: _____)

Name (Mr/Mrs/Ms) _____ Tel _____

Address _____

_____ Fax _____

Please charge the amount of S$ _____ to my VISA/MASTER CARD account (only

Visa/Master Card accepted)

Card No. _____ Card Expiry Date _____

Card Holder's Name (Mr/Mrs/Ms) _____ Signature _____

Send to: ASIAPAC BOOKS PTE LTD 996 Bendemeer Road #06-08/09 Kallang Basin
Industrial Estate Singapore 339944 Tel: (65)3928455 Fax: (65)3926455

 Prices are subject to change without prior notice.

Strategy & Leadership Series (comics)

Sunzi's Art of War:
World's Most Famous Military Classic
This military classic covers widely the subject of strategizing. Its influence is felt not only in state administration, but also in business management, public relations and diplomacy, and even sports. Thus we can see how flexibly Sun Wu's strategizing principles can be applied, making it a resource for anyone desiring to meet any challenge.

Thirty-six Stratagems: Secret Art of War
An outstanding Chinese military classic, the book emphasizes deceptive schemes to achieve military objectives. Examples of the use of these stratagems are marvellously explored by the cartoonist through characters who exhibit ingenuity, bravery, and even folly and calculated brutality in warfare. It has attracted the attention of military authorities and general readers alike.

100 Strategies of War: Brilliant Tactics in Action
Records the numerous battles culled from 21 historical books from the Spring and Autumn Period to the Five Dynasties, spanning more than 1,600 years. The book captures the essence of extensive military knowledge and practice, and explores the use of psychology in warfare, the importance of building diplomatic relations with the enemy's neighbours, the use of espionage and reconnaissance, etc.

Chinese Business Strategies
The Chinese are known for being shrewd businessmen able to thrive under the toughest market conditions. The secret of their success lies in 10 time-tested principles of Chinese entrepreneurship.
This book offers readers 30 real-life, ancient case studies with comments on their application in the context of modern business.

Strategy & Leadership Series (comics)

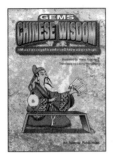

Gems of Chinese Wisdom:
Mastering the Art of Leadership

The book is based on the famous Ming scholar Feng Menglong's 300,000 word masterpiece, *Zhinang*, written to save the country from ruin.

Wise up with this delightful collection of tales and anecdotes on the wisdom of great men and women in Chinese history, including Confucius, Meng Changjun and Gou Jian.

Three Strategies of Huang Shi Gong:
The Art of Government

Reputedly one of man's oldest monograph on military strategy, it was once banned because it was considered too good and deemed to have revealed too many secrets of how the ruler governed the state. The book unmasks the secrets behind brilliant military manoeuvres, clever deployment and control of subordinates, and effective government.

Six Strategies for War:
The Practice of Effective Leadership

Discover the principles employed by Jiang Tai Gong who helped overthrow the despotic Shang rule in ancient China. A powerful book for rulers, administrators and leaders, it covers critical areas in management and warfare including recruiting talents and managing the state; beating the enemy and building an empire; and manoeuvring brilliantly.

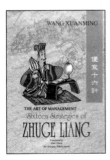

Sixteen Strategies of Zhuge Liang:
The Art of Management

Zhuge Liang, the legendary statesman and military commander during the Three Kingdoms Period, is the epitome of wisdom. Well-grounded in military principles of Sun Zi and other masters before him, he excelled in applying them in state administration and his own innovations, thus winning many spectacular victories.

CHINESE HERITAGE SERIES

Capture the essence of Chinese culture in comics

Enjoy 10% discount and free postage.

Title	Qty	*Price S$	Total
Origins of Chinese Festivals		$14.74	$
Chinese Code of Success: Maxims by Zhu Zi		$14.74	$
Chinese Cuisine		$ 8.99	$
Principles of Feng Shui		$12.51	$
Complete Analects of Confucius Vol 1		$17.61	$
Complete Analects of Confucius Vol 2		$17.61	$
Complete Analects of Confucius Vol 3		$17.61	$

Prices indicated after 10% discount (GST inclusive)
Offer is for readers in Singapore only.

Send this complete page for your mail order

I wish to purchase the above-mentioned titles at the nett price of S$_____

Enclosed is my postal order/money order/cheque/ for S$_____ (No.: _____)

Name (Mr/Mrs/Ms) _____ Tel _____

Address_____

_____ Fax _____

Please charge the amount of S$ _____ to my VISA/MASTER CARD account

(only Visa/Master Card accepted)

Card No._____Card Expiry Date_____

Card Holder's Name (Mr/Mrs/Ms) _____ Signature_____

Send to: ASIAPAC BOOKS PTE LTD 996 Bendemeer Road #06-08/09 Kallang Basin
Industrial Estate Singapore 339944 Tel: (65)3928455 Fax: (65)3926455

Prices are subject to change without prior notice.